The A-List Vocabulary Box Workbook

ISBN: 978-0-615-39998-0

A-List Services LLC
50 E 42nd St, Suite 405
New York, NY 10017
(646) 216-9187
www.alisteducation.com
www.vocabvideos.com

INTRODUCTION TO VOCABULARY

The Critical Reading section of the SAT tests your ability to, well, read critically. This includes your ability to understand the meaning of a complex sentence, your ability to understand an argument, your ability to understand assumptions implicit within a text, your ability to make inferences and deduce the logical consequences of a position, and your vocabulary. Guess which of these skills is the easiest to improve?

In olden times, vocabulary used to be a bigger part of the SAT, but it still counts for a lot. The Sentence Completions are obviously very vocabulary dependent, and they alone account for almost 30% of the section, potentially worth **150 points**.

Vocabulary is important on the Passages, as well. Vocabulary-in-Context questions and Tone questions are often blatantly vocab-dependent, but all questions and their choices may use hard words, and the right answer often hinges on a tricky word. Then there's the passage itself, which is also made up of words, words you'll have to know. Vocabulary is always an important part of reading—if you want to be able to read, you have to know words.

Often, the *only* thing that makes a question hard is its vocabulary. Compare these two questions:

Dave was in a ------- mood; he was smiling and cheerful all day long.

(A) happy
(B) angry
(C) sad
(D) smart
(E) cold

Dave was in a ------- mood; he was smiling and cheerful all day long.

(A) sanguine
(B) bilious
(C) disconsolate
(D) perspicacious
(E) boreal

Did you notice the difference?

Because vocabulary is so important to so many questions, we at A-List have developed a foolproof rule to help you turn the hardest Reading questions into the easiest questions:

LEARN MORE WORDS

That is all.

Luckily, we've got a great way to do that: ***the A-List Vocabulary Box***.

THE VOCABULARY BOX

About the Box

The Vocabulary Box was originally developed as a set of 500 flashcards. This book provides all the same content as those flashcards presented in a convenient workbook format.

The 500 words used in the Vocabulary Box were selected based on a study to determine which words occur most frequently on the SAT. This isn't just a list of words we like or some vocab trivia game where we pull out the hardest words we can find. **We only chose words that have appeared frequently on the SAT**.

The words themselves are **organized according to frequency**. The words at the beginning appear the most frequently, so they are the most important to learn for the SAT.

On the left side of each page you'll find:

- **The word itself**. We refer to these as "boxwords".
- The word's **number** in the box.
- The word's **part of speech** (noun, verb, or adjective).
- An easy-to-read **pronunciation guide**.

> You don't have to memorize the numbers, but whenever we refer to a boxword in the text, we'll put the word's number in parentheses.

On the right you'll find:

- The **definition** of the word. Note that sometimes a boxword may have two different but related definitions.
- An **example sentence** showing the word in use.
- If the word has two definitions with completely different meanings, they are listed on separate lines. An **asterisk** (*) indicates which definition is used in the example sentence.

Some, but not all, words may also have:

- **Synonyms**: A list of other boxwords that have the same meaning as this word
- **Categories**: Sometimes, a group of words in the box have similar or overlapping meanings. We've grouped these into categories with names to help you associate these words with each other. Note that members of a given category may not be *exact* synonyms, but simply have related meanings. See *Appendix C* in this book for a list of all the categories and the words they contain.
- **Word Alerts**: These notes give additional forms of the word, either by changing its part of speech or by adding prefixes or suffixes. They also give information about roots and relationships between boxwords.

Here's an example of a boxword and all its information:

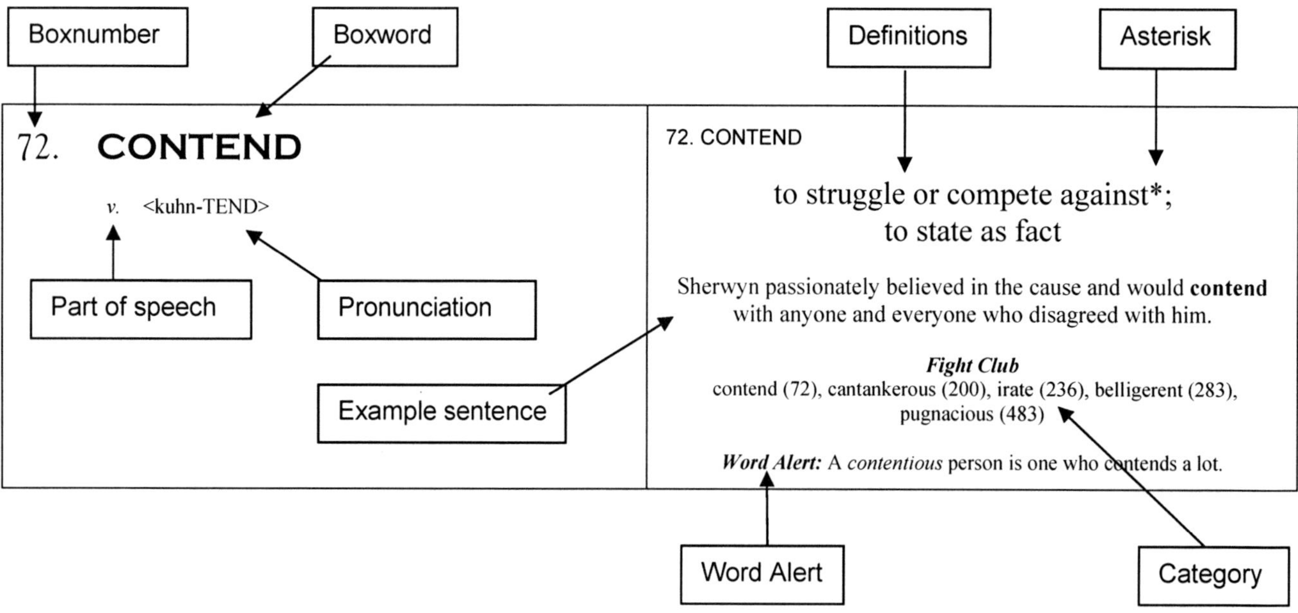

How to use the Box

It's easy to say "learn more words" but it can be hard to actually get started and even harder to make the words stick. There are no right or wrong ways to learn the words. Actually, we take that back; there are definitely *wrong* ways to do it. But there are many different right ways.

Here's a basic outline of how to learn your words. Let's say today's assignment is to learn 10 words:

1. Read through all of that day's words. Make sure you know how to pronounce the word. Read the definition and the sentence. Make sure you understand the definition. Check out any extra information about synonyms or alternate forms. Take notes in the blank space on the left.
2. Quiz yourself. Cover up or fold back the right side of the page, looking only at the words on the right. Guess the definition of each word. Track your performance: either mark whether you got it right in the space below the words or take notes on a separate piece of paper. If you don't know it or if you hesitate—even for a second—put the word in the "don't know" list.
3. Cycle through all the words, then quiz yourself on the "don't know" words. Repeat until they're all in the "know" list.
4. Go through the words one more time to make sure you know them all.

That's basically all there is to it. Here are a few guidelines to help you maximize your box use:

1. Start early, stick to a schedule

The hardest part is to **keep it up**. If you get in the habit of learning words early, you'll have no problem. If you fall behind, it will be that much harder to catch up later.

The most important thing to keep in mind is that this is a large, ongoing project. You cannot cram 500 boxwords at the last minute the night before the SAT. This is a major commitment, and you have to treat it seriously. This is a marathon, not a sprint. **If you fall behind, you will never catch up**.

BUT, if you manage your time, you'll fly through the words in no time.

- You can learn 10 words in 15-20 minutes. If you're quick it could take 10; if you're slow, 30.
- If you learn 10 words a day for 5 days a week, you'll learn 50 a week.
- If you learn 50 words a week, it will take 10 weeks—about two and a half months—to get through the all 500 words.

But what if you don't have 15-20 minutes a day to spare?

<u>That's ridiculous</u>. Everyone can spare 15 minutes a day. Do you know how much time you waste over the course of the day? On your way to school, you could be studying words. Between classes, you could be studying words. Watching TV, during the commercials, you could be studying words. It is incredibly easy to find 15 minutes of downtime during your day, time you can spend studying words. **If you do not study, you will not learn the words.**

2. Write them down

Not everyone learns the same way, so you may find other methods more helpful. If you cycle through the flash cards and the words still don't stick, try **writing the words down**. Get a notebook, take today's words and write down all the key information going across the page: The word, the definition, the sentence, the alternate forms.

Writing everything down will take longer and is more tedious, but the act of writing will cement the word more deeply in your head. And if you use the same notebook each time, by the end you'll have a nice convenient list you can use to review your work.

3. Note different word forms

Remember that when a boxword shows up on the test, it may not look exactly the same as it does on the cards: almost every word in the English can be altered to become another part of speech. Here are a few:

Deride **(77)** means "to speak of with cruelty".	*He derided me in his speech.*
Something *derisive* uses cruel words.	*His derisive speech hurt my feelings.*
Derision is the act of speaking cruelly.	*His speech was full of derision towards me.*
Skeptical **(3)** means "doubting".	*Dave was skeptical about the effectiveness of the pills.*
A *skeptic* is a person who is skeptical.	*Dave is a skeptic about new medications.*
Skepticism is a skeptical attitude.	*Dave responded to your claims with skepticism.*
Temper **(35)** means "to soften or moderate".	*Please temper your emotions: stop shouting.*
Temperance is "moderation or self-control".	*The monk practiced temperance of his desires.*
Temperate means "soft or moderate".	*The climate here is temperate and pleasant.*

Often the card itself will list alternate forms, but not every form is on every card, so you'll have to figure out some of these forms on your own. If you see a word that *really* looks like a boxword, there's a good chance they're related.

4. Notice roots and prefixes

One way to help get the meanings of these words to stick is to look at the *origins* of the words. In every language, words come from other words. Almost every word in English comes from older words that have been broken up, mangled, expanded or rearranged in different ways. So a lot of different words are made up of the same pieces. When they're made up of the same pieces, we can start to notice their relationships.

The little word bits that form the core of the meaning of a word are called *roots*. Sometimes, you'll be able to see the meaning of a word from its roots—you can literally see how the word is a combination of other words. For example, *entrench* **(355)** means "to fix firmly and securely". It literally means to put "*in*" a "*trench*". You can see the meaning right there in the word itself.

Other times, it may not be immediately obvious, but if you learn to recognize common roots, you'll be able to figure out meanings of words you haven't seen before, and you'll be able to remember the meanings of words better. You'll remember a word's meaning better if you understand *why* that's what it means.

Here are a couple of examples of roots that appear in multiple words:

-chron- means "time"	A *chronology* is a time-line.
	Chronological order is when things are ordered in time.
	Chronic **(375)** means "continuing" or "happening all the time".
-verb- means "word"	*Verbal* means having to do with words or speech.
	A *proverb* is a common saying, an expression made up of words.
	Verbose **(412)** means "using lots of words".
-cred- means "believe"	*Credible* **(39)** means "believable".
	Credulous means "tending to believe".

Roots are often changed by adding different **prefixes** to them. Prefixes are little bits that come at the beginning of a word and alter the meaning of the root. The following prefixes all mean "**not**":

in-	*Incredible* means "unbelievable". *Incredulous* (**144**) means "not believing, skeptical".
il- *im-* *ir-*[*]	*Illogical* means "not logical". *Implausible* means "not *plausible* (**27**)". *Irrelevant* means "not relevant".
dis-	A *disadvantage* is something that is *not* an advantage. *Disingenuous* means "not *ingenuous* (**120**)".
non-	*Nonpartisan* means "not *partisan* (**53**)".

Of course, not all prefixes mean "not". Here are a few more:

a- or *an-* means "without"	*Apathetic* (**28**) means "lacking interest or emotion". *Anarchy* means "chaos, lacking government". *Anachronistic* (**170**) means "in the wrong time".
eu- (pronounced like "you") means "good"	*Eulogy* (**303**) is a speech praising someone ("good words"). *Euphonious* means "pleasant sounding" or "harmonious". *Euphemism* (**231**) is a clean (or good) phrase used to describe something dirty. Like "use the restroom" instead of, well, you know...
circum- means "around"	*Circumference* is the path *around* a circle. *Circumvent* (**411**) means to get *around* something, or to avoid. *Circumspect* (**219**) means cautious. "Spect" means "look", so this literally means "look around" (like you're checking for danger).

Knowing a foreign language can help you, too[†]. French, Spanish, and Latin all share a lot of the same roots as English, so your knowledge of those languages can help you pick up on meanings. Observe:

Spanish	*French*	*Meaning*	*Boxword*
fácil	facile	"easy"	*facilitate* (**490**) = to make easy
flor	fleur	"flower"	*florid* (**475**) = elaborately decorated, flowery
bueno	bon	"good"	*benevolent* (**99**) = tending to be good

Some of you are freaking out now, because some of you are even worse at Spanish than you are at English. "What, it's not enough that I'm bad at Reading, I've got to study *Latin* now? Great! I'm doomed!"

Don't freak out. You don't *need* to know all this stuff about roots and prefixes. It *can* help you remember meanings if you see the connections between words. But you're not going to spot them all, and you get no extra points for knowing that "eloquent" and "circumlocution" share a root.

[*] These prefixes are all forms of the "in-" prefix that have changed to make the resulting word more pleasant sounding: *il-* appears before roots starting with *l*, *ir-* before *r*, *im-* before *b*, *m*, and *p*, and *in-* before all other letters.

[†] Well, not *any* language. Just languages related to English. Knowing Japanese or Finnish or Ojibwe probably won't help much.

Just learn the words, any way you can.

5. Use mnemonic devices

Mnemonic* devices are memory tricks you can play to help connect a word and its meaning in your head. People remember things more easily when they have **concrete pictures** to go with them.

- *Undermine* (**6**) means to "weaken". Imagine if you dig a mine under a house; you will weaken the foundation.
- *Gregarious* (**404**) means "sociable". Imagine two people, Greg and Gary, who are the life of the party and are best friends with everyone.
- *Sagacious* (**393**) means "wise". Imagine a very wise, very old monk who lives on the top of a tall mountain. He is so old that his skin is beginning to sag off of his face.

Stupid? Perhaps. But the stupider you make them, the easier they'll be to remember. It's always the really annoying jingles that get stuck in your head for days. The important thing is to make them **memorable**.

6. Review!

It's not enough to learn this week's words just so you'll do well on this week's quiz. (Yes, there will be quizzes.) The point is to remember them *when you take the SAT.* So as you work your way through the box, you should periodically review the words you've already learned. Just flip to a random page from a previous week's assignment, and see if you still remember the words. If you don't, learn them again.

By the way, you do really need to know these words. Not just to do well on the SAT, but to do well at life. These are words in the English language that you will encounter for the rest of your life. Without good command of the language, you may be doomed to a *meager* (**424**) salary at a *mediocre* (**87**) job.

BEYOND THE BOX

Mystery Words

The Box is an essential source of words that you'll need for the SAT. But it isn't a complete source. There are other words in the language and there is a 99.99% chance that you will see words you don't know on the test.† We call those words **Mystery Words**. When you do encounter mystery words, there are a few things to keep in mind:

1. Don't lie to yourself.

Don't pretend you know what it means. If you don't know it, you don't know it. Put a **question mark** next to it. This is a placeholder: "I'm not sure what this word means, so I'll deal with the words I know first and get back to it."

2. Don't eliminate mystery words.

Some kids refuse to choose words they don't know. They'll pick words they *know are wrong* just because they're comfortable with them. You can only eliminate the words you know, not the words you don't.

Deal with the words you know first. If the right answer is a word you know, great, you're done! Move on to the next question. If you eliminate all the words you know, then you'll have to deal with the mysteries.

3. Guess!

Eventually, you're going to find yourself in a situation where you'll have to guess a word you don't know. Remember: if you can eliminate some choices, the odds are in your favor to guess from whatever's left. But how will you know which one to guess? Here are some tips.

---

* Pronounced "Neh-MON-ic". Weirdly, the first "m" is silent. This word comes from a Greek root that means "memory"; the same root appears in *amnesia* which means "lack of memory".

† We will admit there is a 0.01% chance that there is someone reading this whose vocab is so good that he or she will know every word on the test. If that person is you, why are you reading this? Go study some math.

Look for roots.
As discussed above, often you can figure out a word's meaning but looking at its parts. See if any of those words you don't know look like words you do know. Even if you can't figure out exactly what it means, you might still be able to tell the character of a word. For example, if it starts with "eu-", you know it will probably mean something *good*, even though you won't necessarily know in what way it's good.

Beware of false roots.
A lot of the time roots can help you figure out meanings, but sometimes guessing roots can lead you astray. Here are a few examples of words that may not mean what you think*:

- *Inflammable* looks like it means "not flammable", but it actually means "flammable".
- *Indifferent* (**10**) looks like it means "not different", but it actually means "impartial".
- *Judicious* (**353**) looks like it has to do with a courtroom, but it actually means "prudent".
- *Bombastic* (**155**) looks like it has something to do with explosions, but it actually means "using arrogant or pompous speech".

Also note that words you do know might have more than one meaning or use. For example, *exploit* (**108**) can mean "to selfishly take advantage", but it doesn't have to be bad. It can also simply mean "to use advantageously" without a negative connotation.

Be advised that the folks who write the questions know which words kids get confused by, and they will use that against you. In fact, you'll sometimes see a **Fool's Gold** choice on Reading questions: there'll be a choice that's very tempting but actually wrong, because the word doesn't mean what everyone thinks it means. This is why we have Rule 1 above: *Don't lie to yourself* about whether you know a word.†

If all else fails, guess the hardest word.
Because the test makers know that kids are afraid of guessing mystery words, a hard word is more likely to be right than an easy word, especially on a hard question. So if you've got two or three choices left and you have no idea what any of them mean, don't waste time: just pick the word that looks scariest, and move on.

Adding words

As you go through drills and practice tests, you'll encounter some hard words that aren't in the Box. As you do the drills, treat them like mysteries and guess as needed. But later, you'll go over those questions and find out what they mean. Even though they're not in the Box, *you could be learning those words too.*

You can keep track of those words in *Appendix D* at the end of this book. When you encounter a new word, look up the definition in a dictionary. Write the word and its definition in the spaces provided. Then come up with your own example sentence using the word.

And of course, there are all sorts of other places to learn words.‡ You may have gotten other vocabulary books in school. There are vocabulary resources and word-a-day features on the Internet. Crossword puzzles are full of good hard words. You could even just read things. Books, for example. Or even newspapers or magazines. After all, it is possible that you can improve your reading skills by reading more.

---

* These words may seem odd, but their origins do make sense. *Inflammable* comes from *enflame*, which means "to catch fire". *Indifferent* is how you feel if it "makes *no difference*" to you. Being *judicious* is showing good *judgment*. *Bombastic* comes from a French word meaning "cotton wadding"...okay, that one doesn't make much sense.

† Of course, the words listed above are boxwords, so you'll learn their meanings and you won't fall for these traps. The more words you actually *learn*, the less often you'll have to guess.

‡ We encourage you to use other sources to supplement your vocabulary, but don't use other sources *instead* of the Vocabulary Box. Remember that the Box contains words *that frequently appear on the SAT*, so these words should be your number-one priority. If you learn what "epizootic" means, that's great, but you probably won't see it on the test, and it's much more important that you know what "indifferent" means.

THE WORDS

1. **DISMISS**

v. <dis-MIS>

1. DISMISS

to reject

Amy **dismissed** John's attempt to get back together.

Word Alert: Someone *dismissive* tends to dismiss everything.

2. **INNOVATIVE**

adj. <IN-uh-vay-tiv>

2. INNOVATIVE

new and creative

The **innovative** design of this camera will revolutionize the way people take pictures.

Synonyms: novel (58)

Word Alert: To *innovate* is to be innovative. An *innovation* is an innovative creation.

3. **SKEPTICAL**

adj. <SKEP-ti-kuhl>

3. SKEPTICAL

doubting, questioning, not believing

John said that he is over Amy, but Bob is **skeptical** of the claim.

Synonyms: incredulous (144)

Word Alert: A *skeptic* is a skeptical person. *Skepticism* is the state of being skeptical.

4. **PROFOUND**

adj. <pruh-FOUND>

4. PROFOUND

deep; far-reaching

What you do now will have a **profound** impact on your future.

Word Alert: *Profundity* is the state of being profound.

5. **ANECDOTE**

n. <AN-ik-doht>

5. ANECDOTE

a short account of an interesting or humorous incident

Arthur lightened his speech by including some amusing **anecdotes** about his trip to Greece.

6. **UNDERMINE**

v. <un-der-MINE>

6. UNDERMINE

to weaken

John is still in love with Amy and will do everything he can to **undermine** her relationship with Scott.

7. **OBJECTIVE**

adj. <ub-JECK-tiv>

7. OBJECTIVE

not influenced by emotions, unbiased

Rather than making assumptions and jumping to conclusions, the doctor launched an **objective** study to determine whether the drug was effective.

Synonyms: dispassionate (79), impartial (401)

Word Alert: As a noun, objective means *a goal.*

8. **ADVOCATE**

v. <AD-vuh-kate>

8. ADVOCATE

to speak in favor of, promote

All SAT teachers **advocate** learning vocabulary because it is the easiest way to improve one's Reading score.

Synonyms: espouse (459)

Word Alert: *An advocate* is a person who advocates. *Advocacy* is the act of advocating .

9. **NOSTALGIA**

n. <no-STAL-juh>

9. NOSTALGIA

a bittersweet longing for the past

Whenever John looks at old pictures of Amy, he cannot help but feel **nostalgia** for the time they spent together.

Synonyms: wistfulness [wistful (188)]

Word Alert: If you are *nostalgic*, you are experiencing nostalgia.

10. **INDIFFERENT**

adj. <in-DIF-er-ent>

10. INDIFFERENT

having no preference

Marge is **indifferent** about her college choice; she doesn't care where she winds up going.

Synonyms: apathetic (38), nonchalant (161)

Word Alert: This word does NOT mean *not different.*

11. **RESENT**

v. <ri-ZENT>

11. RESENT

to feel angry and bitter about

I **resent** your remarks, jerk!

12. **COMPROMISE**

v. <KOM-pruh-mize>

12. COMPROMISE

to expose to danger or suspicion*;
to mutually settle differences

The governor's past use of drugs **compromised** his credibility.

13. **CYNICAL**

adj. <SIN-ih-cul>

13. CYNICAL

believing that people are motivated by selfishness; pessimistic

Bob is so **cynical** he doesn't even trust his own mother's motives.

Word Alert: A *cynic* is a cynical person who is full of *cynicism*

14. **AESTHETIC**

adj. <ess-THEH-tik>

14. AESTHETIC

concerning beauty

This beautiful new car has great **aesthetic** value, but it doesn't run very well.

Word Alert: An *aesthete* is a person who is very concerned with aesthetic things.
Word Alert: Don't confuse this with *ascetic* (312).

15. **AMBIVALENT**

adj. <am-BIV-uh-lent>

15. AMBIVALENT

having opposing feelings; uncertain

Gary is **ambivalent** about going to Harvard: it is a good school, but he wants to stay in the South.

16. **EVOKE**

v. <ih-VOHK>

16. EVOKE

to summon or call forth

Seeing Amy again **evoked** such painful memories that John began to weep.

17. **DIMINISH**

v. <di-MIN-ish>

17. DIMINISH

to lessen or make smaller

My happiness about winning the class election was **diminished** when I realized how much more work I'd have to do now.

Synonyms: abate (299)

Word Alert: Something *diminutive* is very small.

18. **CONTEMPT**

n. <kuhn-TEMPT>

18. CONTEMPT

a lack of respect and intense dislike

John felt nothing but **contempt** for Scott since he stole Amy away from him.

Bad Blood
contempt (18), disdain (19), scorn (61), antagonistic (136), animosity (357), abhor (403), rancor (410), acrimony (467)

Word Alert: Someone *contemptuous* is full of contempt. Something *contemptible* is worthy of contempt.

19. **DISDAIN**

n. <dis-DAYN>

19. DISDAIN

intense dislike

Because of his **disdain** for Scott, John refuses to speak to him anymore.

Bad Blood
contempt (18), disdain (19), scorn (61), antagonistic (136), animosity (357), abhor (403), rancor (410), acrimony (467)

Word Alert: Disdain can also be a verb meaning *to dislike intensely.*

20. **PRAGMATIC**

adj. <prag-MAT-ik>

20. PRAGMATIC

practical

Holding weekly meetings in Bermuda might be fun, but it would not be a **pragmatic** strategy, Scott.

21. REVERE

v. <ri-VEER>

21. REVERE

to respect, honor or admire

Bob is **revered** by the countless students he has helped get into college.

Synonyms: esteem (232)

Word Alert: *Reverence* is the act of revering.
Word Alert: If the prefix, *ir-* means *not*, what would *irreverence* mean?

---

22. PROVOCATIVE

adj. <pruh-VAWK-uh-tiv>

22. PROVOCATIVE

tending to stir to anger or action

This artist makes **provocative** nude paintings that often shock and offend the public.

Word Alert: To *provoke* is to be provocative.

---

23. INDULGE

v. <in-DUHLJ>

23. INDULGE

to please or satisfy

I know I'm on a diet, but I can't help but **indulge** myself with this chocolate cake.

Word Alert: *Indulgent* means tending to indulge.

---

24. RHETORIC

n. <REH-tuh-ric>

24. RHETORIC

one's use of language (especially effective language)

Caroline's speech was very convincing; her persuasive **rhetoric** made up for her lack of concrete evidence.

Word Alert: *Rhetorical* means having to do with rhetoric.
A *rhetorician* is a person skilled in rhetoric.
Word Alert: A *rhetorical question* is a question that you don't actually want answered; you only asked it for rhetorical effect.

---

25. SCRUTINIZE

v. <SKROOT-in-ize>

25. SCRUTINIZE

to examine carefully

After **scrutinizing** the data for three weeks, I have finally come to a conclusion.

Word Alert: *Scrutiny* is the act of examining. Something *inscrutable* cannot be examined or understood.

26. FOSTER

v. <FAW-ster>

26. FOSTER

to promote the development of

Good reading skills will **foster** good writing skills.

Synonyms: nurture (376)

27. PLAUSIBLE

adj. <PLAW-zuh-buhl>

27. PLAUSIBLE

believable

It's technically possible that the dog did in fact eat your homework, but it is not very **plausible**.

Word Alert: If the prefix, *im-* means *not*, what would *implausible* mean?

28. INACCESSIBLE

adj. <in-uhk-SES-uh-buhl>

28. INACCESSIBLE

not easily approached, entered, or obtained

The fortress is **inaccessible**; no one can get in or out.

29. UNDERSCORE

v. <UN-der-skohr>

29. UNDERSCORE

to emphasize

John tends to yell at his students when he wants to **underscore** something important.

30. AWE

n. (rhymes with "saw")

30. AWE

a mixed emotion of respect, wonder, and dread

Seeing the Grand Canyon for the first time filled Allen with **awe**.

Word Alert: Something that causes awe is *awesome*.

31. SUBSTANTIATE

v. <suhb-STAN-shee-ate>

31. SUBSTANTIATE

to support with proof

Although everyone suspects that it was John who set fire to Scott's car, there is no proof to **substantiate** the claim.

Word Alert: To substantiate is to give *substance* to an argument.

32. CONFORM

v. <kuhn-FORM>

32. CONFORM

to be similar; to adapt

Connor always **conforms** to the latest fads rather than developing his own style.

Like-Minded
conform (32), uniform (73), consensus (88), accord (180), concord (207), concur (279)

Word Alert: When you conform, you put yourself in a state of *conformity*.

33. TRIVIAL

adj. <TRIV-ee-uhl>

33. TRIVIAL

insignificant, unimportant

Historical dates are **trivial** facts; a true understanding of history requires knowledge of why things happen.

Synonyms: inconsequential (157), frivolous (186), negligible (395)

Word Alert: To *trivialize* is to make something seem trivial.

34. INDIGNATION

n. <in-dig-NAY-shun>

34. INDIGNATION

anger (over something unjust)

There is much public **indignation** over the city's plan to tear down the playground in order to build a power plant.

Word Alert: To be *indignant* is to feel indignation.

35. TEMPER

v. <TEM-per>

35. TEMPER

to soften or moderate

If you don't **temper** that attitude of yours I'm going to have to ask you to leave.

Feel Better
temper (35), mollify (203), mitigate (260), alleviate (293), palliative (310)

Word Alert: Something that is temperate is soft or moderate. *Temperance* is moderation or self-control.

36. MUNDANE

adj. <muhn-DAYN>

36. MUNDANE

ordinary, commonplace

Instead of big action or sweeping melodrama, this movie portrays the **mundane** events of everyday life.

Played Out
mundane (36), prosaic (194), banal (221), hackneyed (345), insipid (382), trite (460)

37. VULNERABLE

adj. <VUHL-ner-uh-buhl>

37. VULNERABLE

not protected against harm; easily injured

The best time to strike is when your enemy is most **vulnerable**.

Word Alert: If the prefix *in-* means *not*, what would *invulnerable* mean?

38. APATHETIC

adj. <ap-uh-THET-ik>

38. APATHETIC

lacking interest, concern, or emotion

Apathetic about the SAT, Dick actually fell asleep during the test.

Synonyms: indifferent (10), nonchalant (161)

Word Alert: *Apathy* is an apathetic state of mind.

39. CREDIBLE

adj. <KRED-uh-buhl>

39. CREDIBLE

believable

You can trust her testimony; she's a **credible** witness.

Word Alert: If the prefix *in-* means *not*, what would *incredible* mean?

40. ARBITRARY

adj. <AHR-bi-trer-ee>

40. ARBITRARY

determined by impulse or chance, without reason

Marge was indifferent about her college choice, so she made an **arbitrary** decision.

Unpredictable
arbitrary (40), whimsical (69), capricious (130), erratic (168), impetuous (175), volatile (341), mutable (359), mercurial (387)

41. INHERENT

adj. <in-HEER-uhnt>

41. INHERENT

naturally occurring, essential

Humans have an **inherent** ability to become fluent in any language they are exposed to at a young age.

Synonyms: innate (189)

42. DISPARAGE

v. <di-SPAIR-ij>

42. DISPARAGE

to speak of in an insulting way

I can take gentle teasing, but I will not allow you to **disparage** my mother.

Trash Talk
disparage (42), denounce (66), deride (77), decry (204), belittle (263), deprecate (440), vilify (485)

43. DISCERN

v. <di-SURN>

43. DISCERN

to detect or perceive

A good wine expert can **discern** slight differences in wines that taste the same to most people.

Eagle Eye
discern (43), astute (96), keen (234), perspicacity (384), incisive (480)

Word Alert: To be *discerning* is to be insightful or perceptive.

44. PROSPERITY

n. <pro-SPER-i-tee>

44. PROSPERITY

success; being well-off

After winning the lottery, Penelope went from a life of poverty to a life of **prosperity**.

Word Alert: To *prosper* is to be prosperous and possess *prosperity*.

45. DIGRESS

v. <di-GRES>

45. DIGRESS

to stray from the main subject

Dr. Chen never finishes his lectures on time because he always **digresses** onto other topics.

Word Alert: A *digression* is an act of digressing.

46. **PERPETUAL**

adj. <per-PEH-choo-uhl>

46. PERPETUAL

continuing forever or indefinitely

Kayla was worried that if she didn't go to a good college, she would live in a **perpetual** state of poverty.

Word Alert: To *perpetuate* is to make something perpetual.

47. **ELITIST**

adj. <ih-LEET-ist>

47. ELITIST

believing one is superior (often wrongly)

Roger is an **elitist**; he refuses to talk to anyone who didn't go to an Ivy League school.

Cocky
elitist (47), pretentious (52), condescend (117), grandiose (150), bombastic (155), patronize (356), pompous (452), haughty (463)

Word Alert: *Elite* means superior in status (without the negative connotation); as a noun it means a group that is superior in status.

48. **ASSESS**

v. <uh-SESS>

48. ASSESS

to make a judgment about

I need all the facts before I can **assess** the situation.

49. **PARADOX**

n. <PAIR-uh-doks>

49. PARADOX

a seemingly contradictory statement that may nonetheless be true

"I always lie when I tell the truth," is a **paradox**.

50. **MELANCHOLY**

adj. <MEL-uhn-kaw-lee>

50. MELANCHOLY

sad; gloomy

Kurt has a **melancholy** disposition; he spends all day sulking and writing poems about sadness and death.

Cry Baby
melancholy (50), lament (51), despair (116), morose (284), despondent (443)

Word Alert: Melancholy can also be a noun meaning *sadness*.

51. LAMENT

v. <luh-MENT>

51. LAMENT

to regret; to show grief for

When you get older, you will **lament** your wasted opportunities.

Cry Baby
melancholy (50), lament (51), despair (116), morose (284), despondent (443)

Word Alert: Something *lamentable* is something regrettable.

52. PRETENTIOUS

adj. <prih-TEN-shuhs>

52. PRETENTIOUS

excessively showy;
claiming unjust standing*

Karl **pretentiously** thinks he's more sophisticated than we are because he listens to really obscure music.

Cocky
elitist (47), pretentious (52), condescend (117), grandiose (150), bombastic (155), patronize (356), pompous (452), haughty (463)

Word Alert: A *pretense* is false appearance.

53. PARTISAN

adj. <PAHR-tuh-zuhn>

53. PARTISAN

devoted or biased in support of a group

This sportswriter is **partisan** against my favorite team; he only writes about their failures, never their triumphs

Word Alert: If the prefix *non-* means *not*, what would *nonpartisan* mean?

54. AUTONOMY

n. <aw-TAWN-uh-mee>

54. AUTONOMY

independence

Every high school student dreams of moving away from home to get some **autonomy**.

Word Alert: Someone *autonomous* possesses autonomy.

55. AMBIGUOUS

adj. <am-BIG-yoo-uhs>

55. AMBIGUOUS

vague or unclear

The ending of the movie was **ambiguous**; the audience couldn't definitively tell whether the main character was good or evil.

What the--?
ambiguous (55), equivocal (78), enigmatic (97), esoteric (129), abstruse (247), nebulous (340)

56. **PEDANTIC**

adj. <puh-DAN-tic>

56. PEDANTIC

insisting on following minor rules; overly dry and academic

My teacher is so **pedantic** he cares more about whether I misuse commas in my essays than whether my argument is good.

Word Alert: A *pedant* is someone who is pedantic. *Pedantry* is the act of being pedantic.
Word Alert: The *peda-* root has to do with *teaching*, so *pedagogical* means *related to teaching* but without a negative connotation.

---

57. **COMPLACENT**

adj. <kuhm-PLAY-suhnt>

57. COMPLACENT

self-satisfied to the point of inactivity; unconcerned

The talented athlete grew so **complacent**, he began to skip practice.

Synonyms: smug (184)

---

58. **NOVEL**

adj. <NOV-uhl>

58. NOVEL

strikingly new or different

Bob came up with a **novel** design for a car that is entirely powered by donuts and tacos.

Synonyms: innovative (2)

Word Alert: *Novel* and *innovative* (2) come from the same root.

---

59. **REFUTE**

v. <reh-FYOOT>

59. REFUTE

to disprove

The success of A-List students **refutes** the notion that you cannot improve your SAT score.

Synonyms: debunk (110), repudiate (267)

---

60. **IDIOSYNCRATIC**

adj. <id-ee-oh-sin-KRAT-ik>

60. IDIOSYNCRATIC

peculiar to an individual

Chapman has an **idiosyncratic** habit of always showering in the dark.

Word Alert: An *idiosyncrasy* is an idiosyncratic characteristic or behavior.

61. SCORN

n. (rhymes with "horn")

61. SCORN

intense hatred or disrespect

While John still loves Amy, he feels nothing but **scorn** for Scott, the man who stole her from him.

Bad Blood
contempt (18), disdain (19), scorn (61), antagonistic (136), animosity (357), abhor (403), rancor (410), acrimony (467)

62. OBSOLETE

adj. <OB-suh-leet>

62. OBSOLETE

no longer in use or current

The phonograph is such an **obsolete** device, I bet you don't even know what one is.

Old School
obsolete (62), archaic (276)

63. DISCREDIT

v. <dis-KRED-it>

63. DISCREDIT

to ruin the reputation of

The scandal **discredited** the politician and forced him to resign.

64. INVOKE

v. <in-VOHK>

64. INVOKE

to enforce or put into operation

In order to legally arrest the suspect, the detectives **invoked** a rarely enforced law.

Word Alert: An *invocation* is something that invokes something else.

65. ARTICULATE

adj. <ahr-TIK-yuh-lit>

65. ARTICULATE

using clear and expressive language

Always an **articulate** speaker, Arthur impressed the crowd with his wonderful speech.

Synonyms: eloquent (71)

Word Alert: Articulate can also be a verb meaning *to speak or pronounce distinctly.*

66. **DENOUNCE**

v. <di-NOUNS>

66. DENOUNCE

to condemn openly

The candidate **denounced** the current mayor, blaming him for the increasing crime and excessive tax rates.

Trash Talk
disparage (42), denounce (66), deride (77), decry (204), belittle (263), deprecate (440), vilify (485)

---

67. **DEFER**

v. <di-FUR>

67. DEFER

to submit or yield to another's wish or opinion

I think we should head north, but I will **defer** to you since you are a more experienced hiker.

Word Alert: *Deference* is the act of deferring.

---

68. **FUTILE**

adj. <FYOOT-il>

68. FUTILE

having no useful result

"She doesn't want you, John. Trying to seduce Amy will be **futile**."

---

69. **WHIMSICAL**

adj. <WIM-zi-kuhl>

69. WHIMSICAL

impulsive, fanciful

It was a **whimsical** decision to which he gave little thought.

Unpredictable
arbitrary (40), whimsical (69), capricious (130), erratic (168), impetuous (175), volatile (341), mutable (359), mercurial (387)

Word Alert: A *whim* is a whimsical thought or feeling.

---

70. **INDUCE**

v. <in-DOOS>

70. INDUCE

to bring about the occurrence of

Pregnant women sometimes take drugs to **induce** labor if the child is not born in a reasonable amount of time.

71. ELOQUENT

adj. <EH-lo-quent>

71. ELOQUENT

well spoken

Everyone loved Sarah's speech because she is such an **eloquent** speaker.

Synonyms: articulate (65)

Word Alert: The *-loq-* root means *speech*, so someone *loquacious* is talkative.

---

72. CONTEND

v. <kuhn-TEND>

72. CONTEND

to struggle or compete against*;
to state as fact

Sherwyn passionately believed in the cause and would **contend** with anyone and everyone who disagreed with him.

Fight Club
contend (72), cantankerous (200), irate (236), belligerent (283), pugnacious (483)

Word Alert: A *contentious* person is one who contends a lot.

---

73. UNIFORM

adj. <YOO-nuh-form>

73. UNIFORM

always the same

My mother gives a **uniform** response to every request: “No”.

Like-Minded
conform (32), uniform (73), consensus (88), accord (180), concord (207), concur (279)

---

74. BOLSTER

v. <BOHL-ster>

74. BOLSTER

to support or reinforce

Chapman needed a pep talk to **bolster** his confidence before he gave his speech.

Synonyms: buttress (495)

---

75. COMPETENT

adj. <KOM-pi-tuhnt>

75. COMPETENT

properly or adequately qualified

Esteban may never win a Nobel Prize, but he is still a **competent** scientist and does accurate research.

Word Alert: If the prefix *in-* means *not*, what would *incompetent* mean?

76. **EXTRAVAGANT**

adj. <ek-STRAV-uh-guhnt>

76. EXTRAVAGANT

excessive

John tried to impress Amy with **extravagant** gifts that Scott could not afford.

Overboard
extravagant (76), lavish (159), opulent (346), luxurious (456), exorbitant (471)

77. **DERIDE**

v. <di-RIDE>

77. DERIDE

to speak of or treat with cruelty

Bob is so cruel that he harshly **derided** his student for making a minor careless mistake.

Trash Talk
disparage (42), denounce (66), deride (77), decry (204), belittle (263), deprecate (440), vilify (485)

Word Alert: *Derision* is the act of deriding.
To be *derisive* is to act with derision.

78. **EQUIVOCAL**

adj. <eh-QUI-vo-cal>

78. EQUIVOCAL

uncertain, vague, misleading

The senator always uses **equivocal** language; she thinks that if she doesn't say anything definite, then technically she isn't lying.

What the--?
ambiguous (55), equivocal (78), enigmatic (97), esoteric (129), abstruse (247), nebulous (340)

Word Alert: To *equivocate* is to speak equivocally.
Word Alert: If the prefix *un-* means *not*, what would *unequivocal* mean?

79. **DISPASSIONATE**

adj. <dis-PASH-uh-nit>

79. DISPASSIONATE

not influenced by emotion or bias

A good journalist should report the news **dispassionately** without showing an opinion about the story.

Synonyms: objective (7), impartial (401)

80. **LAUD**

v. <LAWD>

80. LAUD

to praise

The great king was **lauded** by his people almost to the point of being seen as a god.

Hip Hip Hooray!
laud (80), commend (121), extol (245), acclaim (307), adulation (399), exalt (402)

Word Alert: Laud has the same root as *applaud.*

81. **SOLEMN**

adj. <SOL-uhm>

81. SOLEMN

serious and sober

"This is no laughing matter," the judge said **solemnly**. "You are facing a life sentence."

Serious Business
solemn (81), somber (109), earnest (190)

---

82. **HOMOGENEOUS**

adj. <ho-mo-GEE-nee-yus>

82. HOMOGENEOUS

all of the same or similar kind

Arthur travels with a **homogeneous** group of people who all think and look alike.

Word Alert: If the prefix *hetero-* means *different*, what would *heterogeneous* mean?

---

83. **COLLABORATE**

v. <kuh-LAB-uh-rayt>

83. COLLABORATE

to work together

Instead of submitting individual entries, we all **collaborated** on a single project for the contest.

---

84. **ELUSIVE**

adj. <ih-LOO-siv>

84. ELUSIVE

tending to escape

Despite the state-wide manhunt, the **elusive** criminal is still at large.

Gone with the Wind
elusive (84), evasive (172), ephemeral (287), transitory (407), transient (498)

Word Alert: To *elude* is to be elusive.

---

85. **NOTORIOUS**

adj. <no-TAWR-ee-uhs>

85. NOTORIOUS

known widely and unfavorably; famous for something bad

Everyone knows about the **notorious** murder of Biggie Smalls.

Word Alert: *Notoriety* is the state of being notorious.

86. ADMONISH

v. <ad-MON-ish>

86. ADMONISH

to gently criticize or warn

His mother **admonished** Dave to not let his grades slip during his senior year.

Thumbs Down
admonish (86), reproach (112), censure (213), scathing (441), rebuke (457), berate (486)

---

87. MEDIOCRE

adj. <mee-dee-OH-ker>

87. MEDIOCRE

ordinary, so-so

I want to be great, not just **mediocre**.

Word Alert: *Mediocrity* is the state or quality of being mediocre.

---

88. CONSENSUS

n. <kuhn-SEN-suhs>

88. CONSENSUS

general agreement

The **consensus** is clear: we all hate the SAT!

Like-Minded
conform (32), uniform (73), consensus (88), accord (180), concord (207), concur (279)

---

89. ECCENTRIC

adj. <ek-SEN-trik>

89. ECCENTRIC

strange, unconventional

Chapman had a rather **eccentric** habit of talking to his moustache.

Word Alert: An *eccentricity* is an eccentric characteristic.

---

90. RETICENT

adj. <RET-uh-suhnt>

90. RETICENT

restrained or reserved

John was **reticent** at the party and didn't talk to any of the girls.

Tight-Lipped
reticent (90), succinct (132), concise (176), terse (243), laconic (330)

91. ERADICATE

v. <ih-RAD-ih-kayt>

91. ERADICATE

to eliminate

We must **eradicate** these termites before they destroy our house.

92. METICULOUS

adj. <muh-TIK-yoo-luhs>

92. METICULOUS

extremely careful

The detective **meticulously** checked the crime scene for evidence.

Synonyms: conscientious (261), scrupulous (364)

93. EMBELLISH

v. <em-BEL-ish>

93. EMBELLISH

to add fictitious details to*;
to decorate

Bob **embellished** his autobiography so much that it became more fiction than fact.

94. SUPPRESS

v. <suh-PRES>

94. SUPPRESS

to prevent from showing*;
to put down forcibly

Amy can no longer **suppress** her true feelings; she really loves Scott.

Synonyms: quell (201), subdue (209)

95. ORTHODOX

adj. <OR-thuh-doks>

95. ORTHODOX

commonly accepted, traditional

Galileo was denounced for rejecting the **orthodox** belief that the earth is the center of the universe.

96. ASTUTE

adj. <uh-STOOT>

96. ASTUTE

having sharp judgment

The **astute** student noticed that the teacher had made a mistake.

Eagle Eye
discern (43), astute (96), keen (234), perspicacity (384), incisive (480)

97. ENIGMATIC

adj. <en-ig-MAT-ik>

97. ENIGMATIC

puzzling

Bob is an **enigmatic** creature; no one understands why he behaves the way he does.

What the--?
ambiguous (55), equivocal (78), enigmatic (97), esoteric (129), abstruse (247), nebulous (340)

Word Alert: An *enigma* is an enigmatic thing.

98. BENIGN

adj. <buh-NINE>

98. BENIGN

kind or beneficial*;
harmless

The **benign** nurse was caring and gentle, and she eased my suffering during my stay at the hospital

99. BENEVOLENT

adj. <buh-NEV-uh-luhnt>

99. BENEVOLENT

generous, performing kind acts

Bob has always been **benevolent** and gives to charity every year.

Synonyms: magnanimous (152)

100. PROLIFIC

adj. <pruh-LIF-ik>

100. PROLIFIC

producing abundant works or results

Shakespeare was a **prolific** author, having written 40 plays in just 28 years.

101. COHERENT

adj. <co-HEER-ent>

101. COHERENT

logically connected, making sense

The jury was convinced by the attorney's **coherent** argument and let her client go free.

Word Alert: To *cohere* is to make something coherent or to stick together.
Word Alert: If the prefix *in-* means *not*, what would *incoherent* mean?

102. PROVINCIAL

adj. <pruh-VIN-shuhl>

102. PROVINCIAL

narrow-minded

Don't be so **provincial**; try to see the bigger picture.

Synonyms: insular (488)

103. DEARTH

n. <DURTH>

103. DEARTH

a shortage or small amount

The army was ultimately defeated not by their enemies but by the **dearth** of available food during the winter.

Synonyms: paucity (302)

104. EPITOMIZE

v. <ih-PIT-uh-mize>

104. EPITOMIZE

to be a perfect example of

Dave's poor performance on this practice test **epitomizes** why it's important to study vocabulary.

Perfect 10
epitomize (104), paragon (256), exemplar (431)

Word Alert: An *epitome* <ih-PIT-uh-mee> is a perfect example.

105. FLOURISH

v. <FLUR-ish>

105. FLOURISH

to grow well

Bacteria **flourish** in this kind of environment; this entire area will be infected soon.

Synonyms: burgeon (468)

106. **ZEALOUS**

adj. <ZELL-us>

106. ZEALOUS

filled with or motivated by enthusiastic devotion

Gary was a **zealous** vocabulary lover; he studied his box for three hours a night and talked about vocab with everyone he met.

X-treme Intensity!
zealous (106), fervent (250), ardor (253), impassioned (270), galvanize (332)

Word Alert: A *zealot* is a zealous person.
Zeal (rhymes with "seal") is enthusiasm.

---

107. **RECONCILE**

v. <REH-kuhn-sahyl>

107. RECONCILE

to reestablish a close relationship between

Scott wants to **reconcile** his differences with John and go back to being good friends.

Word Alert: *Reconciliation* is the act of reconciling.
Word Alert: Reconcile has the same root as *conciliate* (119).

---

108. **EXPLOIT**

v. <ek-SPLOIT>

108. EXPLOIT

to use fully or take advantage of

Bob is an expert strategist; he always **exploits** his enemy's vulnerabilities.

---

109. **SOMBER**

adj. <SOM-ber>

109. SOMBER

gloomy*;
serious or grave

News of his mother's injuries put Bob in a **somber** mood.

Serious Business
solemn (81), somber (109), earnest (190)

---

110. **DEBUNK**

v. <dih-BUHNK>

110. DEBUNK

to disprove or expose as false

No matter how many people **debunk** them, urban legends continue to be told as if they were true.

Synonyms: refute (59), repudiate (267)

111. ADEPT

adj. <uh-DEPT>

111. ADEPT

very skilled

Bob is an **adept** player; he is his team's MVP every year.

Synonyms: adroit (156)

112. REPROACH

v. <ri-PROHCH>

112. REPROACH

to criticize or express disappointment

The teacher **reproached** me after she discovered that I had been cheating.

Thumbs Down
admonish (86), reproach (112), censure (213), scathing (441), rebuke (457), berate (486)

Word Alert: Reproach can also be a noun meaning *an act of criticism or blame.*

113. EXASPERATE

v. <ig-ZAS-puh-rayt>

113. EXASPERATE

to anger or irritate

Amy was **exasperated** by John; why won't he just leave her alone?

Synonyms: grate (423)

114. REMINISCE

v. <re-mi-NISS>

114. REMINISCE

to recollect and talk about the past

My father, full of nostalgia, loves to **reminisce** about how he met my mother.

Word Alert: *Reminiscence* is the act of reminiscing. Something that is *reminiscent* causes reminiscence.

115. DIVERGENT

adj. <di-VUR-juhnt>

115. DIVERGENT

differing from another; drawing apart from a common point

The twins' lives followed **divergent** paths, with one becoming a doctor and the other becoming a drunken fool.

Word Alert: To *diverge* is to become divergent.
Word Alert: If the prefix *con-* means *together*, what would *convergent* mean?

116. DESPAIR

n. <di-SPAIR>

116. DESPAIR

a complete loss of hope

John felt deep **despair** once he realized that Amy would never come back to him.

Cry Baby
melancholy (50), lament (51), despair (116), morose (284), despondent (443)

Word Alert: Despair can also be a verb meaning *to lose hope.*

117. CONDESCEND

v. <con-duh-SEND>

117. CONDESCEND

to deal with people in a superior manner

Don't take that **condescending** tone with me; you're no better than I am.

Cocky
elitist (47), pretentious (52), condescend (117), grandiose (150), bombastic (155), patronize (356), pompous (452), haughty (463)

118. DEBILITATE

v. <di-BIL-i-tayt>

118. DEBILITATE

to weaken

After suffering a **debilitating** injury, the athlete could not go on.

Synonyms: enervate (400)

119. CONCILIATE

v. <kuhn-SIL-ee-ate>

119. CONCILIATE

to bring peace, to reconcile

The president helped **conciliate** the strained relationship between the two warring nations.

Word Alert: Conciliate has the same root as *reconcile* (107).

120. INGENUOUS

adj. <in-JEN-yoo-uhs>

120. INGENUOUS

innocent, honest and straightforward

The **ingenuous** child gave a simple and honest answer.

Synonyms: candid (124), forthright (417)

Word Alert: If the prefix *dis-* means *not*, what would *disingenuous* mean?

121. COMMEND

v. <kuh-MEND>

121. COMMEND

to praise

The police commissioner **commended** the officer for heroically rescuing the hostage.

Hip Hip Hooray!
laud (80), commend (121), extol (245), acclaim (307), adulation (399), exalt (402)

122. CONVOLUTED

adj. <con-vuh-LOOT-ed>

122. CONVOLUTED

complicated

Stacy gave an unnecessarily **convoluted** explanation for what should be a simple math problem.

123. VERSATILE

adj. <VUR-suh-tahyl>

123. VERSATILE

capable of doing many things well

Bob is a **versatile** player; he can play both offense and defense.

124. CANDID

adj. <KAN-did>

124. CANDID

honest and straightforward

Chapman was unusually **candid** when he told us about everything he did on his vacation to the Virgin Islands.

Synonyms: ingenuous (120), forthright (417)

Word Alert: *Candor* is the quality of being candid.

125. CALLOUS

adj. <KAL-uhs>

125. CALLOUS

emotionally hardened or unfeeling

When John sent Amy a love letter, she **callously** threw it away without even reading it. John wept openly, yet she felt nothing.

126. **CONJECTURE**

n. <kuhn-JEK-cher>

126. CONJECTURE

guesswork

Until we get the test results back, discussing whether John is on steroids is just **conjecture**.

---

127. **AFFLUENT**

adj. <AF-loo-uhnt>

127. AFFLUENT

wealthy

Only the **affluent** could afford to buy such luxurious homes.

---

128. **TENACIOUS**

adj. <tuh-NAY-shuss>

128. TENACIOUS

persistent, determined

Even though they were down by 30 points, the football players **tenaciously** refused to give up.

Pig-Headed
tenacious (128), dogmatic (329), obstinate (337), intransigent (408), dogged (458), obdurate (465),

Word Alert: To have *tenacity* is to be tenacious.

---

129. **ESOTERIC**

adj. <es-uh-TER-ik>

129. ESOTERIC

understood by only a few

The meaning of the word "esoteric" should not be **esoteric**.

What the--?
ambiguous (55), equivocal (78), enigmatic (97), esoteric (129), abstruse (247), nebulous (340)

---

130. **CAPRICIOUS**

adj. <kuh-PREE-shuhs>

130. CAPRICIOUS

impulsive, unpredictable

The **capricious** king constantly changed his mind, making crazy new laws whenever he felt like it.

Unpredictable
arbitrary (40), whimsical (69), capricious (130), erratic (168), impetuous (175), volatile (341), mutable (359), mercurial (387)

Word Alert: A *caprice* is a capricious change of mind.

131. DUBIOUS

adj. <DOO-bee-uhs>

131. DUBIOUS

doubtful, questionable

I am skeptical of your **dubious** claim that you can eat 50 hot dogs in five minutes.

132. SUCCINCT

adj. <suk-SINKT or suh-SINKT>

132. SUCCINCT

precise expression using few words

Haiku is a **succinct** form of poetry, capable of evoking detailed imagery in just three lines.

Tight-Lipped
reticent (90), succinct (132), concise (176), terse (243), laconic (330)

133. RESILIENT

adj. <ri-ZIL-yuhnt>

133. RESILIENT

able to recover promptly

Though exhausted, the **resilient** runner managed to finish the marathon.

134. INCONGRUOUS

adj. <in-CON-grew-us>

134. INCONGRUOUS

inappropriate; inconsistent

His well-mannered behavior was **incongruous** with his reputation for being wild.

135. MANIFEST

v. <MAN-uh-fest>

135. MANIFEST

to show or demonstrate plainly, to reveal

His anger **manifests** itself in obvious ways: he begins to beat his chest and foam at the mouth.

Word Alert: Manifest can also be an adjective meaning *clearly apparent to the mind or senses.*
Word Alert: A *manifesto* is a written document in which you reveal your beliefs.

136. ANTAGONISTIC

adj. <an-tag-uh-NIS-tik>

136. ANTAGONISTIC

hostile

John has always been excessively **antagonistic** towards everyone, not just those who cross him.

Bad Blood
contempt (18), disdain (19), scorn (61), antagonistic (136), animosity (357), abhor (403), rancor (410), acrimony (467)

Word Alert: An *antagonist* is a person who is antagonistic.

137. ALIENATE

v. <AY-lee-uh-nayt>

137. ALIENATE

to make unfriendly or hostile

The mayor **alienated** her biggest supporters when she suddenly switched political parties.

Synonyms: estrange (390)

138. REITERATE

v. <ree-IT-uh-rayt>

138. REITERATE

to repeat

You must study. I **reiterate**: you must study.

139. PRISTINE

adj. <PRIS-teen>

139. PRISTINE

unspoiled, completely pure

His fear of germs made Roger obsessively keep his bathroom in **pristine** condition.

140. EMPIRICAL

adj. <em-PIR-i-kuhl>

140. EMPIRICAL

based on observation or experiment

A scientist should base his conclusions on **empirical** evidence, not on gut feelings.

141. **EMINENT**

adj. <EM-uh-nuhnt>

141. EMINENT

outstanding, distinguished*;
standing out, noticeable

A-List teachers are emerging as **eminent** experts in the field of test preparation.

---

142. **SERENE**

adj. <suh-REEN>

142. SERENE

calm

While sailing slowly down the stream, I felt like I was in a **serene** dream.

Chill
serene (142), tranquil (158), placid (164), composed (454), equanimity (476)

Word Alert: *Serenity* is the state of being serene.

---

143. **HAIL**

v. (rhymes with "mail")

143. HAIL

to greet or welcome*;
to praise

Everyone in the village **hailed** the king as he passed by.

---

144. **INCREDULOUS**

adj. <in-KRE-juh-luhs>

144. INCREDULOUS

disbelieving

The **incredulous** detective refused to believe John's incredible story.

Synonyms: skeptical (3)

Word Alert: Don't confuse this word with *incredible*.
Word Alert: *Credulous* means tending to believe anything.

---

145. **CONFOUND**

v. <kon-FOUND>

145. CONFOUND

to confuse

The inscription on the ancient tomb was written in a strange language that **confounded** even the experts.

Synonyms: obfuscate (193)

146. **APPRENHENSIVE**

adj. <ap-ri-HEN-siv>

146. APPREHENSIVE

fearful

John was so **apprehensive** before his blind date with Becky that he peed his pants.

---

147. **ENUMERATE**

v. <i-NOO-muh-rayt>

147. ENUMERATE

to specify individually, to count

My boss **enumerated** each and every task he expected me to complete.

---

148. **PREVALENT**

adj. <PREH-va-lent>

148. PREVALENT

widespread

Smoking is unfortunately **prevalent** among teenagers.

---

149. **OBLIVIOUS**

adj. <uh-BLIV-ee-uhs>

149. OBLIVIOUS

forgetful;
unaware*

Chapman was **oblivious** to the dangers of hiking and got a severe poison ivy rash as a result.

Word Alert: *Oblivion* is the state of being completely forgotten.

---

150. **GRANDIOSE**

adj. <gran-dee-OHS>

150. GRANDIOSE

incredibly large;
falsely exaggerating one's worth*

Bob has **grandiose** dreams of being king.

Cocky
elitist (47), pretentious (52), condescend (117), grandiose (150), bombastic (155), patronize (356), pompous (452), haughty (463)

151. RESIGNATION

n. <re-zig-NAY-shun>

151. RESIGNATION

submission, acceptance of something as inevitable

The game wasn't over yet, but the players felt **resignation** over the fact that they would not win.

Word Alert: To be *resigned* is to feel resignation.

---

152. MAGNANIMOUS

adj. <mag-NAN-uh-muhs>

152. MAGNANIMOUS

noble and generous in spirit

Scott is a **magnanimous** man and has forgiven John for everything he has done.

Synonyms: benevolent (99)

---

153. BELIE

v. <beh-LYE>

153. BELIE

to represent falsely

John's laughter **belies** the true pain he feels inside.

---

154. EXACERBATE

v. <ex-ASS-er-bate>

154. EXACERBATE

to make more severe

Walking on an injured leg will only **exacerbate** the injury.

---

155. BOMBASTIC

adj. <bom-BAS-tik>

155. BOMBASTIC

using arrogant or pretentious speech

My **bombastic** English teacher uses big words to show off how smart he is, but he never actually says anything meaningful.

Cocky
elitist (47), pretentious (52), condescend (117), grandiose (150), bombastic (155), patronize (356), pompous (452), haughty (463)

Word Alert: Bombastic is also close in meaning to *verbose* (412).

156. **ADROIT**

adj. <uh-DROIT>

156. ADROIT

very skilled

The **adroit** acrobat twirled and whirled through the air.

Synonyms: adept (111)

Word Alert: If the prefix *mal-* means *bad*, what would *maladroit* mean?

157. **INCONSEQUENTIAL**

adj. <in-kon-si-KWEN-shuhl>

157. INCONSEQUENTIAL

unimportant

Your social life is **inconsequential**! Your academic life is all that matters! Now study!

Synonyms: trivial (33), frivolous (186), negligible (395)

Word Alert: *Consequential* means important, or having a consequence.

158. **TRANQUIL**

adj. <TRAN-kwil>

158. TRANQUIL

calm

The lullaby soon lulled the crying baby into a **tranquil** state.

Chill
serene (142), tranquil (158), placid (164), composed (454), equanimity (476)

Word Alert: *Tranquility* is the state of being tranquil. A *tranquilizer* is a drug that makes you tranquil.

159. **LAVISH**

adj. <LAV-ish>

159. LAVISH

excessive; plentiful

Known for his **lavish** lifestyle, the billionaire partied at only the most expensive clubs.

Overboard
extravagant (76), lavish (159), opulent (346), luxurious (456), exorbitant (471)

160. **RESOLUTE**

adj. <REZ-uh-loot>

160. RESOLUTE

firm or determined

A good soldier must be **resolute** in battle and never surrender.

Synonyms: steadfast (197)

161. NONCHALANT

adj. <NON-shah-LONT>

161. NONCHALANT

casually unconcerned

My girlfriend **nonchalantly** said she was fine, but I could tell she was still mad at me.

Synonyms: indifferent (10), apathetic (38)

---

162. PLACID

adj. <PLAS-id>

162. PLACID

calm, quiet

Sitting by this **placid** lake helps me meditate.

Chill
serene (142), tranquil (158), placid (164), composed (454), equanimity (476)

---

163. OPPORTUNE

adj. <op-er-TOON>

163. OPPORTUNE

suitable, occurring at an appropriate time

Because prices are so low, this is an **opportune** time to buy a house.

Word Alert: An *opportunity* is an opportune circumstance.
An *opportunist* is someone who (selfishly) seizes opportunities.

---

164. DILIGENT

adj. <DIL-i-juhnt>

164. DILIGENT

hard working

You must be **diligent** in your study of vocabulary: learn new words every night!

Synonyms: assiduous (489)

---

165. SUPPLANT

v. <suh-PLANT>

165. SUPPLANT

to take the place of

John still hopes to **supplant** Scott and be the only man in Amy's life.

166. **MANDATE**

n. <MAN-dayt>

166. MANDATE

an authoritative command

When my master issues a **mandate**, I must obey.

Word Alert: A mandate is something that is *mandatory*.

---

167. **PROLIFERATE**

v. <pruh-LIF-uh-rayt>

167. PROLIFERATE

to increase or spread at a rapid rate

The disease **proliferated** uncontrollably and literally ate almost his entire body.

---

168. **ERRATIC**

adj. <ih-RAT-ik>

168. ERRATIC

irregular

Chapman's **erratic** behavior led us to believe he was having trouble with his personal life.

Unpredictable
arbitrary (40), whimsical (69), capricious (130), erratic (168), impetuous (175), volatile (341), mutable (359), mercurial (387)

---

169. **INSOLENT**

adj. <IN-suh-luhnt>

169. INSOLENT

disrespectfully arrogant

The **insolent** soldier told his commanding officer to shut up.

Synonyms: audacity (378)

---

170. **ANACHRONISTIC**

adj. <uh-nak-ruh-NIS-tik>

170. ANACHRONISTIC

in the wrong time period

Missiles in a movie about Mozart would be **anachronistic**.

Word Alert: An *anachronism* is something that is anachronistic.

171. GUILE

n. <GUYL>

171. GUILE

skillful deceit

Using **guile** and a smile, the hustler tricked me out of my life savings.

Shady
guile (171), duplicity (191), cunning (362), treachery (372)

172. EVASIVE

adj. <ih-VAY-siv>

172. EVASIVE

tending to escape;
intentionally vague*

When we accused Dave of cheating, he gave an **evasive** response without confirming or denying the charge.

Gone with the Wind
elusive (84), evasive (172), ephemeral (287), transitory (407), transient (498)

Word Alert: To *evade* means to escape.
Word Alert: Evasive is also similar in meaning to *equivocal* (78).

173. DISPOSITION

n. <dis-puh-ZIH-shuhn>

173. DISPOSITION

one's usual mood

John has a sour **disposition**; he always seems to be unhappy about something.

174. PRECARIOUS

adj. <pri-KAIR-ee-uhs>

174. PRECARIOUS

dangerously unstable or insecure

I'm in a **precarious** position right now; I'm holding on with just one finger.

175. IMPETUOUS

adj. <im-PET-choo-uhs>

175. IMPETUOUS

impulsive, unthinking

The **impetuous** child always acts on his first desire without considering the consequences.

Unpredictable
arbitrary (40), whimsical (69), capricious (130), erratic (168), impetuous (175), volatile (341), mutable (359), mercurial (387)

176. **CONCISE**

adj. <kuhn-SICE>

176. CONCISE

expressing much in few words

A well-crafted sentence should be **concise** and free of unnecessary repetition.

Tight-Lipped
reticent (90), succinct (132), concise (176), terse (243), laconic (330)

---

177. **INHIBIT**

v. <in-HIB-it>

177. INHIBIT

to hold back; to restrain

John's fear of rejection **inhibits** his ability to meet other women.

Road Block
inhibit (177), hinder (183), thwart (272), hamper (297), encumbrance (301), impede (418)

---

178. **WARY**

adj. <WAIR-ee> (rhymes with "hairy")

178. WARY

on guard, cautious, watchful

Be **wary** of strangers who offer you candy.

Synonyms: vigilant (398)

---

179. **RECLUSIVE**

adj. <ri-KLOOS-iv>

179. RECLUSIVE

seeking or preferring isolation

The **reclusive** author always refuses to give interviews about his work.

Word Alert: A *recluse* is someone who is reclusive.

---

180. **ACCORD**

n. <uh-KORD>

180. ACCORD

agreement

After signing the treaty, the leaders of the two countries shook hands as a sign of their new **accord**.

Like-Minded
conform (32), uniform (73), consensus (88), accord (180), concord (207), concur (279)

Word Alert: Accord can also be a verb meaning *to agree*.

181. **PERVASIVE**

adj. <per-VAY-siv>

181. PERVASIVE

spread throughout

There is a **pervasive** smell of curry in my apartment caused by the Indian restaurant downstairs.

Word Alert: To *pervade* is to be pervasive.

---

182. **ENCOMPASS**

v. <en-KUHM-puhs>

182. ENCOMPASS

to enclose; to include

This course **encompasses** everything that you will need to know for the SAT.

---

183. **HINDER**

v. <HIN-der>

183. HINDER

to be or get in the way of

Don't let your emotions **hinder** your judgment; think before you act.

Road Block
inhibit (177), hinder (183), thwart (272), hamper (297), encumbrance (301), impede (418)

Word Alert: A *hindrance* is something that hinders.

---

184. **SMUG**

adj. (rhymes with "bug")

184. SMUG

self-satisfied (especially in a mocking way)

A **smug** grin crept over Lucy's face as she knew she had won the argument.

Synonyms: complacent (57)

---

185. **CONCEDE**

v. <kuhn-SEED>

185. CONCEDE

to admit something is true, often reluctantly

John has finally **conceded** that he will never win back Amy's love.

Word Alert: A *concession* is the act of conceding.

186. **FRIVOLOUS**

adj. <FRIV-uh-luhs>

186. FRIVOLOUS

unworthy of serious attention, unimportant

You've got me working on a **frivolous** assignment; give me something important to do!

Synonyms: trivial (33), inconsequential (157), negligible (395)

Word Alert: A *frivolity* is something that is frivolous.

187. **EMULATE**

v. <EM-yuh-layt>

187. EMULATE

to equal through imitation

Before developing a style of their own, young actors often try to **emulate** the greats who came before them.

188. **WISTFUL**

adj. <WIST-ful>

188. WISTFUL

full of sad desire

Allen **wistfully** thought about his lost love and the life he could have had with her.

Synonyms: nostalgic [nostalgia (9)], melancholy (50)

189. **INNATE**

adj. <ih-NAYT>

189. INNATE

inborn

Some people have to work hard to do well at math while others have an **innate** talent for it.

Synonyms: inherent (41)

190. **EARNEST**

adj. <ER-nest>

190. EARNEST

showing deep sincerity or seriousness

His **earnest** commitment to improving his SAT scores impressed even me.

Serious Business
solemn (81), somber (109), earnest (190)

191. DUPLICITY

n. <doo-PLIS-i-tee>

191. DUPLICITY

deception, deceit

The con artist lived a life of **duplicity**, always making up new scams and new lies.

Shady
guile (171), duplicity (191), cunning (362), treachery (372)

Word Alert: Someone that has duplicity is *duplicitous*.

192. EXPEDITE

v. <EK-spi-dite>

192. EXPEDITE

to speed the progress of

Maybe if we hire more employees we can **expedite** the project.

193. OBFUSCATE

v. <AHB-fuh-skate>

193. OBFUSCATE

to confuse or make obscure

The candidate intentionally **obfuscated** his proposal so the voters wouldn't realize he was calling for a massive tax hike.

Synonyms: confound (145)

194. PROSAIC

adj. <pro-ZAY-ic>

194. PROSAIC

lacking in imagination; dull

His **prosaic** performance in the play was uninspiring and unmemorable.

Played Out
mundane (36), prosaic (194), banal (221), hackneyed (345), insipid (382), trite (460)

195. REVOKE

v. <ri-VOHK>

195. REVOKE

to void by recalling, reversing, or withdrawing

Bob's license was **revoked** after he failed to appear in court.

196. **RENOUNCE**

v. <ri-NOUNCE>

196. RENOUNCE

to reject, disown, or formally give up

I **renounce** my claims to the throne; I no longer want to be king.

Synonyms: relinquish (255)

Word Alert: A *renunciation* in an act of renouncing.

197. **STEADFAST**

adj. <STED-fast>

197. STEADFAST

determined;
firm and dependable*

A **steadfast** friend, Scott has always got my back.

Synonyms: resolute (160)

198. **CACOPHONY**

n. <kuh-KOFF-o-nee>

198. CACOPHONY

jarring, disagreeable sound

The **cacophony** of the streets of New York drove me nuts, so I moved to a quiet farm in Kansas.

Noise Pollution
cacophony (198), strident (246), tumultuous (350), obstreperous (389), boisterous (390)

Word Alert: Something *cacophonous* sounds like a cacophony.
Word Alert: If the prefix *eu-* means *good*, what would *euphony* mean?

199. **THERAPEUTIC**

adj. <thair-uh-PYOO-tik>

199. THERAPEUTIC

having healing powers

That massage really had a **therapeutic** effect on my aching muscles.

200. **CANTANKEROUS**

adj. <can-TANK-er-uhs>

200. CANTANKEROUS

ill-tempered

That **cantankerous** old man is always looking for an argument.

Fight Club
contend (72), cantankerous (200), irate (236), belligerent (283), pugnacious (483)

201. **QUELL**

v. <KWEL>

201. QUELL

to put down forcibly

The police had to use tear gas to **quell** the rioting protesters.

Synonyms: suppress (94), subdue (209)

---

202. **AUSTERE**

adj. <aw-STEER>

202. AUSTERE

strict in discipline; without decoration

The monk lived an **austere** life of simplicity.

Synonyms: ascetic (312)

---

203. **MOLLIFY**

v. <MOL-uh-fye>

203. MOLLIFY

to soften, to ease the anger of

I tried to **mollify** the angry child by giving him a lollypop.

Feel Better
temper (35), mollify (203), mitigate (260), alleviate (293), palliative (310)

---

204. **DECRY**

v. <di-CRY>

204. DECRY

to condemn openly

Bob viciously **decried** his opponent's ideas during the debate.

Trash Talk
disparage (42), denounce (66), deride (77), decry (204), belittle (263), deprecate (440), vilify (485)

---

205. **ALTRUISTIC**

adj. <al-troo-IS-tik>

205. ALTRUISTIC

unselfishly concerned for the welfare of others

Giving all your lottery winnings to charity is an **altruistic** act.

Word Alert: *Altruism* is altruistic behavior.

206. CORRORBORATE

v. <kuh-ROB-uh-rayt>

206. CORROBORATE

to strengthen or support with evidence

Bob claims he was at the bar that night, and he has several witnesses to **corroborate** that.

---

207. CONCORD

n. <KON-kord>

207. CONCORD

agreement

As a sign of their **concord**, everyone signed the contract.

Like-Minded
conform (32), uniform (73), consensus (88), accord (180), concord (207), concur (279)

---

208. ILLUSORY

adj. <ih-LOO-zuh-ree>

208. ILLUSORY

based on or producing illusion; deceptive

"I thought she really loved me; but it was all **illusory**," Scott said.

---

209. SUBDUE

v. <sub-DOO>

209. SUBDUE

to bring under control; to make less intense

The doctors had to use a straitjacket to **subdue** the wild patient.

Synonyms: suppress (94), quell (201),

---

210. SOLICITOUS

adj. <suh-LIH-si-tuhs>

210. SOLICITOUS

anxious or concerned*;
eager

Dave just had a case of the sniffles, but his **solicitous** parents made him go to the emergency room.

211. ECLECTIC

adj. <e-KLEK-tik>

211. ECLECTIC

having elements from a variety of sources

Lester has an **eclectic** taste in music; he listens to everything from Hayden to hip-hop.

---

212. EBULLIENT

adj. <eh-BOO-lee-ent>

212. EBULLIENT

enthusiastic, lively

The bubbly girl was so **ebullient** that I felt invigorated by talking to her.

Party Hearty!
ebullient (212), exuberant (227)

---

213. CENSURE

v. <SEN-sher>

213. CENSURE

to criticize severely

Lauren was **censured** by the committee for her misconduct.

Thumbs Down
admonish (86), reproach (112), censure (213), scathing (441), rebuke (457), berate (486)

Word Alert: Censure can also be a noun meaning *harsh criticism*.

---

214. AVERSE

adj. <uh-VURS>

214. AVERSE

reluctant

Sorry, but I am **averse** to eating bugs.

Word Alert: Don't confuse this word with *adverse* [see adversity (368)].

---

215. DIFFIDENCE

n. <DIF-ih-duhns>

215. DIFFIDENCE

a lack of self-confidence, shyness

John's **diffidence** is obvious; whenever a girl tries to speak to him, he starts biting his nails.

216. JUXTAPOSE

v. <JUHK-stuh-pohz>

216. JUXTAPOSE

to place side by side

Las Vegas is a place of contrasts: a bustling city of lights **juxtaposed** with an empty, desolate desert.

217. VENERATE

v. <VEN-uh-rayt>

217. VENERATE

to respect

In order to show that they **venerate** him, John's students always bow before him.

Word Alert: Something *venerable* is worthy of veneration.

218. GENIAL

adj. <JEEN-ee-uhl>

218. GENIAL

friendly, cheerful

When Gene throws a party, he is always **genial** and welcoming to all his guests.

BFF
genial (218), amiable (262), affable (306), cordial (334), camaraderie (358), amicable (421)

Word Alert: *Congenial* also means friendly or sociable.

219. CIRCUMSPECT

adj. <SUR-kuhm-spekt>

219. CIRCUMSPECT

cautious and wise

The **circumspect** inspector analyzed all the possible clues before determining the killer's identity.

Wise Guy
circumspect (219), discreet (222), prudent (336), judicious (353), shrewd (366), sagacious (393)

220. ASCERTAIN

v. <ASS-er-tain>

220. ASCERTAIN

to find out definitely

I am trying to **ascertain** how and why this has happened.

221. BANAL

adj. <buh-NAL or BAY-nul>

221. BANAL

ordinary and commonplace

This **banal** movie was no different than every other romantic comedy ever made.

Played Out
mundane (36), prosaic (194), banal (221), hackneyed (345), insipid (382), trite (460)

222. DISCREET

adj. <di-SKREET>

222. DISCREET

prudent in speech or act, able to keep a secret

Scott had to be **discreet** when he was out with Amy so John wouldn't see them together.

Wise Guy
circumspect (219), discreet (222), prudent (336), judicious (353), shrewd (366), sagacious (393)

Word Alert: *Discretion* is the quality of being discreet.
Word Alert: Don't confuse this word with *discrete* (430).

223. CONDONE

v. <kuhn-DOHN>

223. CONDONE

to excuse or overlook

I don't normally **condone** this kind of behavior, but I'll allow it just this once.

224. STOIC

adj. <STOW-ik>

224. STOIC

seemingly unaffected by pleasure or pain

Thanks to his meditation, John now remains **stoic** under pressure and is no longer a slave to his anger.

225. DAUNT

v. <DAWNT>

225. DAUNT

to intimidate or lessen one's courage

I was going to go bungee jumping, but I was **daunted** once I saw the height of the bridge.

Word Alert: Someone who is *undaunted* is not afraid.

226. **ORNATE**

adj. <or-NAYT>

226. ORNATE

excessively decorated

My grandmother gave me an **ornate** antique jewelry box that has intricate patterns carved on all sides.

Flashy
ornate (226), flamboyant (244), garish (374), florid (475)

227. **EXUBERANT**

adj. <ig-ZOO-ber-uhnt>

227. EXUBERANT

lively

When the team won the game in the final seconds, an **exuberant** cry came up from the crowd.

Party Hearty!
ebullient (212), exuberant (227)

228. **PERSEVERE**

v. <pur-suh-VEER>

228. PERSEVERE

to be persistent, refuse to stop

There are a lot of words in the vocab box, but you must **persevere** to the end!

229. **RUDIMENTARY**

adj. <roo-duh-MEN-tuh-ree>

229. RUDIMENTARY

being or involving basic facts or principles

If you master all the **rudimentary** mathematical rules, then more advanced concepts will be much easier.

230. **INDIGENOUS**

adj. <in-DIH-jen-us>

230. INDIGENOUS

native

Native Americans are the only people **indigenous** to North America.

231. EUPHEMISM

n. <YOO-fuh-mi-zm>

231. EUPHEMISM

the substitution of inoffensive term for one considered offensive

"Vertically challenged" is a **euphemism** for short.

232. ESTEEM

v. <ih-STEEM>

232. ESTEEM

to value highly, to respect

A-List teachers are **esteemed** wherever they go for their unbounded knowledge and expertise.

Synonyms: revere (21)

Word Alert: Esteem can also be a noun meaning *respect.*

233. OMINOUS

adj. <OM-uh-nuhs>

233. OMINOUS

menacing; threatening

"You will regret not studying," said John in an **ominous** tone.

234. KEEN

adj. <KEEN>

234. KEEN

sharp, perceptive*;
enthusiastic

The A-List team is a **keen** SAT-solving machine.

Eagle Eye
discern (43), astute (96), keen (234), perspicacity (384), incisive (480)

235. CARNIVOROUS

adj. <kar-NIV-er-uhs>

235. CARNIVOROUS

meat-eating

Because it had large, pointy teeth, we believe this dinosaur was **carnivorous.**

236. **IRATE**

adj. <eye-RAYT>

236. IRATE

enraged

John became **irate** when he first learned that Scott was dating Amy.

Fight Club
contend (72), cantankerous (200), irate (236), belligerent (283), pugnacious (483)

---

237. **DISPARITY**

n. <di-SPAIR-i-tee>

237. DISPARITY

the state of being different

The **disparity** between the rich and poor in this country is astounding.

Synonyms: discrepancy (288)

Word Alert: Something *disparate* possesses a disparity.

---

238. **INNOCUOUS**

adj. <in-NOK-yoo-us>

238. INNOCUOUS

harmless

It was an **innocuous** comment that wasn't meant to hurt anybody's feelings.

---

239. **DOCILE**

adj. <DOSS-uhl>

239. DOCILE

easily managed or taught

The animals at this zoo are quite **docile**; you can walk right up and pet them.

Synonyms: tractable (248)

---

240. **ITINERANT**

adj. <eye-TIN-uh-runt>

240. ITINERANT

traveling from place to place; wandering

Tommy is an **itinerant** salesman, traveling from city to city across the midwest selling car parts wherever he goes.

Word Alert: An *itinerary* is a list of all the places you'll be traveling.

241. LUCID

adj. <LOO-sid>

241. LUCID

clear

Thanks to Arthur's **lucid** explanation, that problem no longer seems confusing to me.

Word Alert: To *elucidate* (371) is to make something lucid.

242. EFFUSIVE

adj. <ih-FYOO-siv>

242. EFFUSIVE

overflowing (usually referring to emotions)

Donna is such a drama queen; she makes an **effusive** display whenever she can't get her way.

243. TERSE

adj. <TURS>

243. TERSE

expressing much in few words

A **terse** man, my grandfather only speaks when necessary.

Tight-Lipped
reticent (90), succinct (132), concise (176), terse (243), laconic (330)

244. FLAMBOYANT

adj. <flam-BOY-uhnt>

244. FLAMBOYANT

highly elaborate; showy

Known for her **flamboyant** attire, Sarah wore a bright red wedding dress.

Flashy
ornate (226), flamboyant (244), garish (374), florid (475)

245. EXTOL

v. <ek-STOHL>

245. EXTOL

to praise

John was so obsessed with Amy that he constantly **extolled** her virtues.

Hip Hip Hooray!
laud (80), commend (121), extol (245), acclaim (307), adulation (399), exalt (402)

246. **STRIDENT**

adj. <STREYE-dunt>

246. STRIDENT

harsh, loud

Donna is a **strident** debater, making her point through shouting rather than persuasion.

Noise Pollution
cacophony (198), strident (246), tumultuous (350), obstreperous (389), boisterous (390)

247. **ABSTRUSE**

adj. <ab-STROOS>

247. ABSTRUSE

difficult to understand

I thought I understood how to do the problem, but your **abstruse** explanation confused me more.

What the--?
ambiguous (55), equivocal (78), enigmatic (97), esoteric (129), abstruse (247), nebulous (340)

248. **TRACTABLE**

adj. <TRAK-tuh-buhl>

248. TRACTABLE

easily managed, led, or taught

The teacher was pleased to find that his new students were **tractable** and not disruptive.

Synonyms: docile (239)

Word Alert: If the prefix *in-* means *not*, what would *intractable* mean?

249. **ILLICIT**

adj. <ih-LIS-it>

249. ILLICIT

not permitted by custom or law

She committed an **illicit** act and now must be punished.

Word Alert: Don't confuse this word with *elicit*, which means to evoke (16).

250. **FERVENT**

adj. <FUR-vuhnt>

250. FERVENT

greatly emotional or enthusiastic

I am so **fervently** in love with her, I feel feverish!

X-treme Intensity!
zealous (106), fervent (250), ardor (253), impassioned (270), galvanize (332)

Word Alert: *Fervor* is a fervent feeling.

251. AMALGAM

n. <uh-MAL-gum>

251. AMALGAM

a combination of diverse elements

The Star Wars movies are an **amalgam** of traditional science fiction movies, westerns, and Japanese samurai legends.

Word Alert: To *amalgamate* is to make an amalgam.

252. PENCHANT

n. <PEN-chunt>

252. PENCHANT

preference or tendency

Allen has a **penchant** for strange hats and never leaves the house without wearing something on his head.

Synonyms: predilection (391), propensity (394)

253. ARDOR

n. <AHR-der>

253. ARDOR

energy, intensity, enthusiasm

John was once overwhelmed by the **ardor** of his love for Amy, but that love has now faded.

X-treme Intensity!
zealous (106), fervent (250), ardor (253), impassioned (270), galvanize (332)

Word Alert: Someone *ardent* is full of ardor.

254. JADED

adj. <JAY-ded>

254. JADED

weary, worn out

After having been in so many failed relationships, Amy is now **jaded**.

255. RELINQUISH

v. <ri-LIN-kwish>

255. RELINQUISH

to give up; to release

The captain was forced to **relinquish** control of the ship to the mutinous crew.

Synonyms: renounce (196)

256. **PARAGON**

n. <PAIR-uh-gone or PAIR-uh-gun>

256. PARAGON

a model of perfection

Arthur is a **paragon** of good sportsmanship; he is always friendly and polite with his opponents, even after his toughest losses.

Perfect 10
epitomize (104), paragon (256), exemplar (431)

257. **EXONERATE**

v. <eg-ZON-uh-rayt>

257. EXONERATE

to free from blame or responsibility

"I am not guilty of arson and I will be **exonerated** of this charge," said John.

Synonyms: vindicate (321)

258. **FLAGRANT**

adj. <FLAY-gruhnt>

258. FLAGRANT

obviously bad or offensive

Bringing cookies for the teacher was a **flagrant** attempt to get on his good side before he graded the essays.

259. **DISSEMINATE**

v. <di-SEM-uh-nayt>

259. DISSEMINATE

to spread widely

To get back at Amy, John has been **disseminating** ugly rumors about her.

260. **MITIGATE**

v. <MIT-ih-gayt>

260. MITIGATE

to lessen in force or intensity

This headgear and mouthpiece should **mitigate** any pain you feel in the boxing ring.

Feel Better
temper (35), mollify (203), mitigate (260), alleviate (293), palliative (310)

261. CONSCIENTIOUS

adj. <con-shee-EN-shuhs>

261. CONSCIENTIOUS

thorough and careful*;
guided by your conscience

A **conscientious** employee always does the job right.

Synonyms: meticulous (92), scrupulous (364)

262. AMIABLE

adj. <AY-mee-uh-buhl>

262. AMIABLE

friendly

Always an **amiable** fellow, Amos treats everyone like a best friend.

BFF
genial (218), amiable (262), affable (306), cordial (334), camaraderie (358), amicable (421)

263. BELITTLE

v. <bi-LIT-il>

263. BELITTLE

to speak of in an insulting way

Even a little **belittling** can still hurt someone's feelings.

Trash Talk
disparage (42), denounce (66), deride (77), decry (204), belittle (263), deprecate (440), vilify (485)

264. JOCULAR

adj. <JOCK-yuh-lur>

264. JOCULAR

joking

Bob has a **jocular** personality; he has a witty remark for every situation and nothing he says is ever fully serious.

265. DECORUM

n. <di-KOHR-uhm>

265. DECORUM

correct or appropriate behavior

When at a wedding or a funeral, it is necessary to act with some **decorum**.

Word Alert: To be *decorous* is to act with decorum.

266. DISGRUNTLED

adj. <dis-GRUHN-tuld>

266. DISGRUNTLED

unhappy

The **disgruntled** employee's grumbling grew louder and louder.

---

267. REPUDIATE

v. <ri-PYOO-dee-ate>

267. REPUDIATE

to reject the validity of

John **repudiated** the accusation that he is stalking Amy; he says he's just trying to be friendly.

Synonyms: refute (59), debunk (110)

---

268. OPAQUE

adj. <oh-PAKE>

268. OPAQUE

not clearly understood*;
impenetrable by light, dense

His essay was so **opaque** that I wasn't even sure what it was supposed to be about.

Word Alert: *Opacity* is the state of being opaque.

---

269. CAJOLE

v. <kuh-JOHL>

269. CAJOLE

to persuade by flattery

Dave tried to **cajole** his boss into giving him a raise by complimenting him on his generosity.

---

270. IMPASSIONED

adj. <im-PASH-uhnd>

270. IMPASSIONED

filled with passion

The general made an **impassioned** speech to his troops before leading them into battle.

X-treme Intensity!
zealous (106), fervent (250), ardor (253), impassioned (270), galvanize (332)

271. **ENTICE**

v. <en-TICE>

271. ENTICE

to lure or tempt

Commercials try to **entice** you to buy their products by playing on your fears and desires.

272. **THWART**

v. (rhymes with "wart")

272. THWART

to stop or prevent

The security system successfully **thwarted** the thief's attempt to break into the house.

Road Block
inhibit (177), hinder (183), thwart (272), hamper (297), encumbrance (301), impede (418)

273. **DEMEAN**

v. <di-MEEN>

273. DEMEAN

to lower in status or worth

You really **demean** yourself when you publicly suck up to your boss like that, John.

274. **COMPEL**

v. <kuhm-PEL>

274. COMPEL

to exert a strong, irresistible force on

Her desperate cries of pain **compelled** me to help her.

275. **COMPLICITY**

n. <kuhm-PLIS-i-tee>

275. COMPLICITY

participation in a bad act or a crime

Since you drove the getaway car, your **complicity** in the robbery is irrefutable.

276. **ARCHAIC**

adj. <ar-KAY-ik>

276. ARCHAIC

outdated; really old

The catapult is an **archaic** weapon; no one has used one in centuries.

Old School
obsolete (62), archaic (276)

Word Alert: If *-ology* means *study of* then what would *archeology* mean?

277. **OBTUSE**

adj. <uhb-TOOS>

277. OBTUSE

lacking intellect

He's a bit **obtuse**; you have to explain things to him slowly.

278. **LANGUID**

adj. <LANG-gwid>

278. LANGUID

lacking energy or spirit

Feeling lazy and **languid**, I sat on the couch watching television all day

Word Alert: *Languor* is the state of being languid.

279. **CONCUR**

v. <kuhn-KUR>

279. CONCUR

to agree

We all **concur** with the details of the contract

Like-Minded
conform (32), uniform (73), consensus (88), accord (180), concord (207), concur (279)

280. **SUPERFLUOUS**

adj. <soo-PER-floo-us>

280. SUPERFLUOUS

extra, unnecessary

If you rid yourself of **superfluous** material things and live an austere life, you will find inner peace.

Synonyms: gratuitous (414)

281. **SANGUINE**

adj. <SAN-gwin>

281. SANGUINE

cheerful

A few glasses of sangria always make me feel **sanguine**.

Happy Camper
sanguine (281), felicity (319), euphoria (354), ecstasy (365), elated (442), buoyant (449), mirth (481)

282. **POIGNANT**

adj. <POIN-yuhnt>

282. POIGNANT

touching

It's a **poignant** story that is sure to make you cry.

283. **BELLIGERENT**

adj. <buh-LIH-jer-uhnt>

283. BELLIGERENT

eager to fight

The **belligerent** boxer punched his own trainer.

Fight Club
contend (72), cantankerous (200), irate (236), belligerent (283), pugnacious (483)

Word Alert: The *belli-* root means *combat.* So *bellicose* means *hostile or warlike.*

284. **MOROSE**

adj. <muh-ROHS>

284. MOROSE

gloomy

John is still **morose** over losing Amy; he holds her picture close to his heart before going to sleep.

Cry Baby
melancholy (50), lament (51), despair (116), morose (284), despondent (443)

285. **TACT**

n. (rhymes with "fact")

285. TACT

sensitivity in dealing with others

Always act with **tact** when consoling a victim of a tragedy.

286. **COHESIVE**

adj. <koh-HEE-siv>

286. COHESIVE

sticking or holding together

By the end of the season, all the players came together to form a truly **cohesive** team.

Word Alert: To *cohere* means to stick together. *Coherent* (101) comes from the same root.

287. **EPHEMERAL**

adj. <eh-FEE-muh-ral>

287. EPHEMERAL

lasting for a brief time

Emotions can be **ephemeral**; one day Amy loved John and the next day she felt nothing.

Gone with the Wind
elusive (84), evasive (172), ephemeral (287), transitory (407), transient (498)

288. **DISCREPANCY**

n. <di-SKREP-uhn-see>

288. DISCREPANCY

lack of agreement

The IRS would like you to explain this **discrepancy** of $1000 between your personal records and your tax return.

Synonyms: disparity (237)

289. **ARID**

adj. <A-rid>

289. ARID

dry

This **arid** air is making my skin dry.

290. **ESTRANGE**

v. <ih-STRANGE>

290. ESTRANGE

to cause to become unfriendly or hostile

Amy has managed to **estrange** every man in her life; everyone she's ever dated hates her now.

Synonyms: alienate (137)

291. CONSTITUENT

n. <kuhn-STITCH-oo-uhnt>

291. CONSTITUENT

a component*;
a person that an elected official represents

Each of the **constituents** of this chemical is harmless, but together they make a dangerous explosive.

Word Alert: To *constitute* something is to be a constituent of it.

292. WARRANT

v. <WAR-uhnt>

292. WARRANT

to justify

Given the amount of evidence against him, his arrest was **warranted**.

293. ALLEVIATE

v. <uh-LEE-vee-ate>

293. ALLEVIATE

to make more bearable

Ice is often used to **alleviate** joint pain.

Feel Better
temper (35), mollify (203), mitigate (260), alleviate (293), palliative (310)

294. CIRCUMSCRIBE

v. <sir-cum-SCRIBE>

294. CIRCUMSCRIBE

to limit, restrict, or strictly define*;
to draw a border around

The interview with the candidate was severely **circumscribed**: the host could only ask questions from the pre-approved list of topics.

295. CLANDESTINE

adj. <clan-DEHS-tin>

295. CLANDESTINE

secret (often for illegal acts)

The clan had to hold **clandestine** meetings for fear the government would discover their plot.

Synonyms: surreptitious (361)

296. **TACIT**

adj. <TASS-it>

296. TACIT

implied without being said

Karl and I never actually talk about it, but we have a **tacit** agreement to help each other when one of us needs money.

Word Alert: Someone who is *taciturn* says very little.

297. **HAMPER**

v. <HAM-per>

297. HAMPER

to prevent the movement or action of

The diaper he wore clearly **hampered** his movement; he waddled instead of walked.

Road Block
inhibit (177), hinder (183), thwart (272), hamper (297), encumbrance (301), impede (418)

298. **IMPUGN**

v. <im-PYOON>

298. IMPUGN

to attack as false or wrong, to challenge or question

You are wrong, Mr. President; and I will continue to **impugn** you for as long as you hold office!

299. **ABATE**

v. <uh-BATE>

299. ABATE

to lessen in severity

Dave wanted to cross the street to get a sandwich, but he waited until the rain **abated** so he wouldn't get soaked.

Synonyms: diminish (17)

300. **OBSEQUIOUS**

adj. <ub-SEE-quee-us>

300. OBSEQUIOUS

excessively respectful

Mr. Johnson was annoyed by all his **obsequious** assistants and yes-men who followed him around everywhere, praising every move he made.

Synonyms: ingratiating (323)

301. **ENCUMBRANCE**

n. <en-CUM-bruns>

301. ENCUMBRANCE

a burden

Dave packed his article with so many footnotes that they became an **encumbrance** to understanding his argument.

Road Block
inhibit (177), hinder (183), thwart (272), hamper (297), encumbrance (301), impede (418)

Word Alert: To *encumber* is to be a burden.
Word Alert: If the prefix *dis-* means *not*, what would *disencumber* mean?

302. **PAUCITY**

n. <PAW-sih-tee>

302. PAUCITY

scarcity, a small amount or number

Bob criticized Dave's argument because of the **paucity** of evidence supporting his conclusion.

Synonyms: dearth (103)

303. **EULOGY**

n. <YOO-luh-jee>

303. EULOGY

a written or spoken tribute (usually for someone who has died)

Larry's speech was a moving **eulogy** for a great man.

Word Alert: The prefix *eu-* means *good*, so eulogy literally means *good words*.

304. **PRESCIENT**

adj. <PRESH-unt or PREE-shunt>

304. PRESCIENT

accurately predicting, having knowledge beforehand

Karl's broker gave him **prescient** advice about what stocks to buy, and now he's a millionaire.

Synonyms: clairvoyant [clairvoyance (426)]

Word Alert: The *-scie-* root has to do with *knowledge*. Can you think of other words with this root?

305. **AUGMENT**

v. <awg-MENT>

305. AUGMENT

to increase, to make larger

Chapman tried to **augment** his income by working overtime and getting a second job.

306. AFFABLE

adj. <AF-uh-buhl>

306. AFFABLE

friendly

Becky was worried about her blind date with John, but she found him to be pleasant and **affable**.

BFF
genial (218), amiable (262), affable (306), cordial (334), camaraderie (358), amicable (421)

307. ACCLAIM

v. <uh-KLAYM>

307. ACCLAIM

to praise

The singer's new album was **acclaimed** by many critics as the best album of the year

Hip Hip Hooray!
laud (80), commend (121), extol (245), acclaim (307), adulation (399), exalt (402)

308. ALACRITY

n. <uh-LAK-ri-tee>

308. ALACRITY

eagerness, enthusiasm

Allen always shows up for work with **alacrity**, ready to face the day and do the best job he can.

309. PRODIGIOUS

adj. <pruh-DIH-juhs>

309. PRODIGIOUS

enormous; extraordinary

I have such a **prodigious** amount of work; I'll never get it all done.

Synonyms: copious (379), voluminous (493)

310. PALLIATIVE

adj. <PAL-ee-uh-tiv>

310. PALLIATIVE

tending to ease or relieve

Dr. Steve said that while these pills may not totally cure my disease, they will have a **palliative** effect on my symptoms.

Feel Better
temper (35), mollify (203), mitigate (260), alleviate (293), palliative (310)

311. NEFARIOUS

adj. <nuh-FAIR-ee-us>

311. NEFARIOUS

evil

If we don't stop Dr. Collosso from carrying out his **nefarious** plans, he will surely destroy the world!

312. ASCETIC

adj. <uh-SET-ic>

312. ASCETIC

denying oneself pleasure and luxury

Donna decided to live an **ascetic** life and threw away all her possessions.

Synonyms: austere (202)

Word Alert: The practice of being ascetic is *asceticism*. Ascetic can also be a noun meaning *one who is ascetic*.
Word Alert: Don't confuse this word with *aesthetic* (14).

313. REDOLENT

adj. <RED-uh-lunt>

313. REDOLENT

suggestive*;
having a strong smell

This small English village is **redolent** of an earlier age; I almost expected a knight on horseback to come trotting down the main street.

Synonyms: reminiscent [reminisce (114)], evocative [evoke (16)]

314. CATHARTIC

adj. <kuh-THAR-tik>

314. CATHARTIC

emotionally cleansing or relieving

I find that punching a punching bag after a hard day's work has a **cathartic** effect on me.

315. ENTHRALL

v. <en-THRAWL>

315. ENTHRALL

to hold spellbound, captivate

When I first saw her, I was so **enthralled** by her beauty that I stopped in the middle of the street just to get a look at her.

316. **MODICUM**

n. <MOD-ih-cum>

316. MODICUM

a small amount

Even after such a persuasive argument, I still had a **modicum** of doubt: a tiny part of me just couldn't accept Caroline's conclusion.

317. **PERTINENT**

adj. <PUR-ti-nuhnt>

317. PERTINENT

exactly relevant

Peter rarely speaks in class, but when he does his comments are always perfectly **pertinent** to the discussion.

318. **IMPERIOUS**

adj. <im-PEER-ee-uhs>

318. IMPERIOUS

arrogantly authoritative or overbearing

"Do as I say!" Arthur **imperiously** commanded.

319. **FELICITY**

n. <fuh-LIS-ih-tee>

319. FELICITY

great happiness*;
a well-suited or appropriate style

There was a feeling of great **felicity** in the air at the wedding.

Happy Camper
sanguine (281), felicity (319), euphoria (354), ecstasy (365), elated (442), buoyant (449), mirth (481)

Word Alert: Something *felicitous* is happy or well suited.

320. **INSTIGATE**

v. <IN-sti-gate>

320. INSTIGATE

to stir up

Disparaging someone's mother will usually **instigate** a fight.

Synonyms: provoke [see provocative (22)]

321. **VINDICATE**

v. <VIN-di-kayt>

321. VINDICATE

to clear of blame or suspicion

Chapman's reputation was **vindicated** once he proved that he did not steal the jewels.

Synonyms: exonerate (257)

---

322. **HEDONISTIC**

adj. <hee-dun-ISS-tic>

322. HEDONISTIC

valuing pleasure over all else

Dave lived a **hedonistic** life and spent all of his time eating chocolate sauce straight from the bottle.

Synonyms: indulgent [indulge (23)]

Word Alert: A *hedonist* is one who only values pleasure.

---

323. **INGRATIATING**

adj. <in-GRAY-she-ay-ting>

323. INGRATIATING

pleasing, (especially to gain advantage)

Donna always becomes friendly and **ingratiating** whenever she's about to ask me for money.

Synonyms: obsequious (300)

---

324. **ONEROUS**

adj. <ON-er-us or OH-ner-us>

324. ONEROUS

burdensome

Having defeated Dr. Collosso, we now face the **onerous** task of cleaning up the huge mess caused by our mighty battle.

Synonyms: exacting (439)

Word Alert: An *onus* is a burden.

---

325. **CONVIVIAL**

adj. <kuhn-VIV-ee-uhl>

325. CONVIVIAL

festive, sociable

Connie is a **convivial** creature, always seeking to meet new people.

Synonyms: gregarious (404)

326. PERNICIOUS

adj. <per-NISH-uhs>

326. PERNICIOUS

deadly or destructive

The disease had a **pernicious** effect; it single-handedly killed an entire species.

Killer
pernicious (326), deleterious (380), bane (473)

327. INSINUATE

v. <in-SIN-yoo-ate>

327. INSINUATE

to hint or suggest subtly

Without directly accusing him, the detective **insinuated** that John was to blame for the accident.

328. SQUANDER

v. <SKWON-der>

328. SQUANDER

to waste

Penelope has **squandered** all her lottery winnings and is back in the poor house.

329. DOGMATIC

adj. <dog-MAT-ic>

329. DOGMATIC

stubbornly and arrogantly opinionated

Don't try to argue politics with my father; he's so **dogmatic** you'll never change his mind.

Pig-Headed
tenacious (128), dogmatic (329), obstinate (337), intransigent (408), dogged (458), obdurate (465),

Word Alert: *Dogma* is the set of beliefs that a dogmatic person holds.

330. LACONIC

adj. <luh-KON-ik>

330. LACONIC

using few words (often rudely or mysteriously)

The **laconic** stranger sits at the bar every night nursing his whiskey and brushing off any attempt at conversation.

Tight-Lipped
reticent (90), succinct (132), concise (176), terse (243), laconic (330)

331. DIVISIVE

adj. <di-VICE-iv>

331. DIVISIVE

creating disagreement or dissent

Gary has a **divisive**, critical attitude at a time when we should all be working as a team.

Synonyms: discordant [see discord (499)]

Word Alert: Divisive comes from the same root as *divide*.

332. GALVANIZE

v. <GAL-vuh-nize>

332. GALVANIZE

to stimulate

His inspiring and impassioned speech **galvanized** me to act!

X-treme Intensity!
zealous (106), fervent (250), ardor (253), impassioned (270), galvanize (332)

333. VAPID

adj. <VAP-id>

333. VAPID

lacking liveliness or interest; dull

This **vapid** conversation is rapidly boring me.

334. CORDIAL

adj. <KOR-juhl>

334. CORDIAL

friendly, warm, polite

One should always be **cordial** at social gatherings of any kind.

BFF
genial (218), amiable (262), affable (306), cordial (334), camaraderie (358), amicable (421)

335. SPURIOUS

adj. <SPYOOR-ee-uhs>

335. SPURIOUS

not genuine; false

I find it impossible to believe you now because you've made so many **spurious** claims in the past.

Synonyms: specious (494)

336. **PRUDENT**

adj. <PROO-dent>

336. PRUDENT

wise; careful

If we had been more **prudent** with our money, our business would have succeeded.

Wise Guy
circumspect (219), discreet (222), prudent (336), judicious (353), shrewd (366), sagacious (393)

Word Alert: If the prefix *im-* means *not*, what would *imprudent* mean?

337. **OBSTINATE**

adj. <OB-stuh-nit>

337. OBSTINATE

stubborn

I pleaded with my parents to let me keep the stray dog, but they **obstinately** refused.

Pig-Headed
tenacious (128), dogmatic (329), obstinate (337), intransigent (408), dogged (458), obdurate (465),

338. **DISPEL**

v. <dis-SPEL>

338. DISPEL

to rid of

The instructor's safety demonstration **dispelled** all of my concerns about the danger of bungee jumping. I'm ready to go!

339. **ERUDITE**

adj. <ER-yoo-dite>

339. ERUDITE

scholarly, well educated

Using these vocabulary words in casual conversation can make you seem incredibly **erudite**.

Word Alert: *Erudition* means knowledge or learning.

340. **NEBULOUS**

adj. <NEB-yuh-luhs>

340. NEBULOUS

hazy, vague, or confused; lacking defined form

I'm not sure exactly what he wants; he only gave me **nebulous** orders.

What the--?
ambiguous (55), equivocal (78), enigmatic (97), esoteric (129), abstruse (247), nebulous (340)

341. **VOLATILE**

adj. <VOL-uh-tuhl>

341. VOLATILE

explosive*;
tending to change

These two countries have a **volatile** relationship that could erupt into war at any moment.

Unpredictable
arbitrary (40), whimsical (69), capricious (130), erratic (168), impetuous (175), volatile (341), mutable (359), mercurial (387)

---

342. **VICARIOUS**

adj. <vye-CAIR-ee-us>

342. VICARIOUS

felt or undergone as if one were taking part in the experience or feelings of another

Since Jenny never made it as an actress, she lived **vicariously** through her daughter's successful acting career.

---

343. **WAVER**

v. <WAY-ver>

343. WAVER

to be unsure or weak

Amy is **wavering** between Scott and John; she is unsure who she wants to be with.

Synonyms: vacillate (461)

---

344. **DETER**

v. <di-TUR>

344. DETER

to prevent or discourage from acting

A scarecrow is intended to **deter** crows from eating crops.

Word Alert: A *deterrent* is something used to deter.

---

345. **HACKNEYED**

adj. <HACK-need>

345. HACKNEYED

overused

That comic uses the same **hackneyed** jokes over and over again.

Played Out
mundane (36), prosaic (194), banal (221), hackneyed (345), insipid (382), trite (460)

346. **OPULENT**

adj. <OP-yuh-luhnt>

346. OPULENT

rich or superior in quality

Penelope decorated her mansion with only the most **opulent** things, from the most expensive silks to solid gold furniture.

Overboard
extravagant (76), lavish (159), opulent (346), luxurious (456), exorbitant (471)

---

347. **IMPECCABLE**

adj. <im-PEK-uh-buhl>

347. IMPECCABLE

perfect

The officer was promoted because of his **impeccable** service record.

---

348. **POLARIZE**

v. <POH-luh-rize>

348. POLARIZE

to set at opposite ends or extremes

The issue **polarized** the political party into two warring groups: those who favored the plan and those who didn't.

Word Alert: To be *polar* is to be at opposite ends.

---

349. **DISSENT**

n. <di-SENT>

349. DISSENT

disagreement

As expected, the Democrats' plan was met with **dissent** from the Republicans.

Word Alert: Dissent can also be a verb meaning *to disagree*.

---

350. **TUMULTUOUS**

adj. <too-MUHL-choo-uhs>

350. TUMULTUOUS

disorderly, noisy, turbulent

The **tumultuous** rioters could be heard for miles.

Noise Pollution
cacophony (198), strident (246), obstreperous (389), boisterous (390)

Word Alert: A *tumult* is a tumultuous occurrence.

351. **CONTRIVED**

adj. <kuhn-TRAHYVD>

351. CONTRIVED

obviously planned or made up

Not only is my father a compulsive liar, but he tells stories that are so **contrived** that no one could possibly believe them.

352. **INQUISITIVE**

adj. <in-KWIZ-i-tiv>

352. INQUISITIVE

showing curiosity, asking questions

A good scientist has an **inquisitive** disposition, always questioning why things are the way they are.

353. **JUDICIOUS**

adj. <joo-DISH-uhs>

353. JUDICIOUS

having good judgment, prudent

Punching the President was not a **judicious** move.

Wise Guy
circumspect (219), discreet (222), prudent (336), judicious (353), shrewd (366), sagacious (393)

354. **EUPHORIA**

n. <yoo-FOR-ee-a>

354. EUPHORIA

a feeling of great happiness

Jamie was filled with **euphoria** when she saw how much her SAT score had increased.

Happy Camper
sanguine (281), felicity (319), euphoria (354), ecstasy (365), elated (442), buoyant (449), mirth (481)

Word Alert: To be *euphoric* is to feel euphoria.

355. **ENTRENCH**

v. <en-TRENCH>

355. ENTRENCH

to fix firmly or securely

He's been doing things his way for a long time; his habits are deeply **entrenched**.

356. **PATRONIZE**

v. <PAY-truh-nize>

356. PATRONIZE

to treat condescendingly*;
to support or sponsor

My math teacher constantly **patronizes** us; he talks to us like we're idiots because thinks he's the smartest man alive.

Cocky
elitist (47), pretentious (52), condescend (117), grandiose (150), bombastic (155), patronize (356), pompous (452), haughty (463)

---

357. **ANIMOSITY**

n. <an-uh-MOS-i-tee>

357. ANIMOSITY

bitter hostility

They have so much **animosity** between them that they behave like bloodthirsty animals around each other.

Bad Blood
contempt (18), disdain (19), scorn (61), antagonistic (136), animosity (357), abhor (403), rancor (410), acrimony (467)

---

358. **CAMARADERIE**

n. <com-RAH-der-ee>

358. CAMARADERIE

goodwill among friends

There was a feeling of **camaraderie** among the students that made them truly enjoy coming to class.

BFF
genial (218), amiable (262), affable (306), cordial (334), camaraderie (358), amicable (421)

---

359. **MUTABLE**

adj. <MYOO-tuh-buhl>

359. MUTABLE

subject to change

This region has incredibly **mutable** weather patterns; I never know if it's going to be sweltering hot or freezing cold.

Unpredictable
arbitrary (40), whimsical (69), capricious (130), erratic (168), impetuous (175), volatile (341), mutable (359), mercurial (387)

Word Alert: If the prefix *im-* means *not*, what would *immutable* mean?

---

360. **CONSTRAIN**

v. <kuhn-STRAYN>

360. CONSTRAIN

to restrict*;
to force or compel

There are a lot of repairs I'd like to make to the house, but I am **constrained** by my lack of money.

Word Alert: A *constraint* is something that constrains.

361. SURREPTITIOUS

adj. <sur-uhp-TISH-uhs>

361. SURREPTITIOUS

done or made by secret or stealthy means

Dave has **surreptitiously** been providing information about our company's inner workings to our rivals.

Synonyms: clandestine (295)

362. CUNNING

adj. <KUHN-ing>

362. CUNNING

clever, sneaky

The **cunning** cat burglar could break into even the most well protected buildings.

Shady
guile (171), duplicity (191), cunning (362), treachery (372)

Word Alert: Cunning can also be a noun meaning *skillful deception.*

363. VINDICTIVE

adj. <vin-DIK-tiv>

363. VINDICTIVE

seeking revenge

John still wants "payback"; he is on a **vindictive** mission.

364. SCRUPULOUS

adj. <SKROO-pyuh-luhs>

364. SCRUPULOUS

thorough and careful

Allen is so careful with his collection of porcelain figurines that he **scrupulously** cleans each piece every day.

Synonyms: meticulous (92), conscientious (261)

365. ECSTASY

n. <EK-stuh-see>

365. ECSTASY

intense joy or delight

Amy makes me feel so good, when I'm with her, I'm in **ecstasy**.

Happy Camper
sanguine (281), felicity (319), euphoria (354), ecstasy (365), elated (442), buoyant (449), mirth (481)

Word Alert: If you are *ecstatic* you are filled with ecstasy.

366. **SHREWD**

adj. <SHROOD>

366. SHREWD

smart in a sneaky or tricky manner

The entrepreneur made some **shrewd** moves and now his business is flourishing.

Wise Guy
circumspect (219), discreet (222), prudent (336), judicious (353), shrewd (366), sagacious (393)

367. **STAGNANT**

adj. <STAG-nuhnt>

367. STAGNANT

not moving, flowing, or developing

If you do not practice then your skills will become **stagnant**.

Word Alert: To *stagnate* is to become stagnant.

368. **ADVERSITY**

n. <ad-VUR-si-tee>

368. ADVERSITY

great hardship

Jay has lived a life of **adversity**, from growing up penniless in an orphanage to losing both his legs in a tractor accident.

Word Alert: *Adverse* means harmful or contrary.

369. **PLIABLE**

adj. <PLY-uh-buhl>

369. PLIABLE

flexible

This cookie cutter is made of a **pliable** metal, so you can bend it into any shape you'd like.

Word Alert: *Pliant* also means easily bendable or flexible.

370. **PROPAGATE**

v. <PROP-uh-gayt>

370. PROPAGATE

to transmit or cause to broaden or spread

The politician **propagated** her new ideas for reform by using television, radio, and newspaper promotions.

Word Alert: *Propaganda* is information that is propagated for the purpose of promoting some cause.

371. ELUCIDATE

v. <ih-LOO-si-dayt>

371. ELUCIDATE

to make clear

This book **elucidates** Einstein's theories so effectively that after reading it I feel like I could be a physicist.

Word Alert: To elucidate something is to make it *lucid* (241).

372. TREACHERY

n. <TRECH-uh-ree>

372. TREACHERY

deliberate betrayal of trust

Stealing your best friend's wife is an act of **treachery** that cannot be forgiven.

Shady
guile (171), duplicity (191), cunning (362), treachery (372)

373. HERETICAL

adj. <huh-REHT-i-kul>

373. HERETICAL

characterized by departure from accepted beliefs or standards

Bob's insistence on celebrating Christmas in the nude is **heretical** to me.

Word Alert: A *heretic* is someone who holds heretical opinions (like Bob).

374. GARISH

adj. <GAIR-ish>

374. GARISH

flashy, tastelessly loud and brightly colored

Her dress is so **garish**, just looking at it makes my eyes hurt.

Flashy
ornate (226), flamboyant (244), garish (374), florid (475)

375. CHRONIC

adj. <KRON-ic>

375. CHRONIC

continuing or lingering

Jay has a **chronic** problem that won't go away.

376. **NURTURE**

v. <NUR-cher>

376. NURTURE

to help develop, to nourish

Parents have a responsibility to **nurture** their children.

Synonyms: foster (26)

377. **VEILED**

adj. <VAYLD>

377. VEILED

concealed or disguised

Some have argued that the government's new security laws are just a **veiled** attempt to gain more power.

378. **AUDACITY**

n. <aw-DAS-i-tee>

378. AUDACITY

fearless daring;
disrespectful boldness*

I cannot believe the **audacity** of these children who dare to question my authority!

Synonyms: insolence [see insolent (169)]

Word Alert: Someone *audacious* acts with audacity.

379. **COPIOUS**

adj. <KOH-pee-uhs>

379. COPIOUS

plentiful, abundant

Thanks to the new fertilizer, we've had an incredibly **copious** harvest this year.

Synonyms: prodigious (309), voluminous (493)

380. **DELETERIOUS**

adj. <del-uh-TEER-ee-us>

380. DELETERIOUS

harmful

The most **deleterious** consequence of drug abuse is death.

Killer
pernicious (326), deleterious (380), bane (473)

381. HARANGUE

n. <huh-RANG>

381. HARANGUE

a long, angry speech

Chapman's **harangue** about the importance of recycling gave me a headache.

Word Alert: Harangue can also be a verb meaning *to speak or write in an angry or violent manner*.

382. INSIPID

adj. <in-SIP-id>

382. INSIPID

lacking flavor or zest; dull

This **insipid** food needs some hot sauce.

Played Out
mundane (36), prosaic (194), banal (221), hackneyed (345), insipid (382), trite (460)

383. INCONTROVERTIBLE

adj. <in-kon-truh-VUR-tuh-buhl>

383. INCONTROVERTIBLE

impossible to dispute

It is an **incontrovertible** fact that a good vocabulary is an asset, both on the SAT and in life.

384. PERSPICACITY

n. <pur-spi-KAS-i-tee>

384. PERSPICACITY

a high level of perception or understanding

Because of the amazing **perspicacity** he has shown, we made him the executive vice president of the company.

Eagle Eye
discern (43), astute (96), keen (234), perspicacity (384), incisive (480)

Word Alert: A *perspicacious* person possesses perspicacity.

385. DIVULGE

v. <di-VUHLJ>

385. DIVULGE

to make known, reveal

The witness refused to **divulge** the identity of the killer.

386. **CURTAIL**

v. <ker-TAYL>

386. CURTAIL

to cut short

In order to make time for her studies, Courtney **curtailed** the time she spent with her boyfriend.

387. **MERCURIAL**

adj. <mer-KYOOR-ee-uhl>

387. MERCURIAL

changeable or erratic in mood

Amy is a **mercurial** woman; she loves you one moment then hates you the next.

Unpredictable
arbitrary (40), whimsical (69), capricious (130), erratic (168), impetuous (175), volatile (341), mutable (359), mercurial (387)

388. **TEDIOUS**

adj. <TEE-dee-uhs>

388. TEDIOUS

tiresomely long or boring

Counting sheep is a **tedious** act.

Word Alert: *Tedium* is the quality of being tedious.

389. **OBSTREPEROUS**

adj. <uhb-STREP-er-uhs>

389. OBSTREPEROUS

noisily and stubbornly defiant

The chanting strikers **obstreperously** blocked the entrance to the building.

Noise Pollution
cacophony (198), strident (246), tumultuous (350), obstreperous (389), boisterous (390)

390. **BOISTEROUS**

adj. <BOY-ster-uhs>

390. BOISTEROUS

noisy; disorderly

The **boisterous** boy beat his drums all day and night.

Noise Pollution
cacophony (198), strident (246), tumultuous (350), obstreperous (389), boisterous (390)

391. **PREDILECTION**

n. <pred-ih-LEK-shuhn>

391. PREDILECTION

a preference; a tendency toward favoring

She seems to have a **predilection** for chili powder; she puts too much of it in everything she cooks.

Synonyms: penchant (252), propensity (394)

---

392. **INUNDATE**

v. <in-UHN-dayt>

392. INUNDATE

to overwhelm with*;
to flood

I feel **inundated** by all these vocabulary words!

---

393. **SAGACIOUS**

adj. <suh-GAY-shuhs>

393. SAGACIOUS

insightful and wise

She is **sagacious** and always offers good advice.

Wise Guy
circumspect (219), discreet (222), prudent (336), judicious (353), shrewd (366), sagacious (393)

Word Alert: A *sage* is a sagacious person. *Sagacity* is the quality of being sagacious.

---

394. **PROPENSITY**

n. <pruh-PEN-si-tee>

394. PROPENSITY

tendency

Given John's **propensity** for violence, I don't think he should lead the peacekeeping mission.

Synonyms: penchant (394), predilection (391)

---

395. **NEGLIGIBLE**

adj. <NEG-li-juh-buhl>

395. NEGLIGIBLE

insignificant; really small

A 10-point change in your SAT score is **negligible** and will not affect your college admission.

Synonyms: trivial (33), inconsequential (157), frivolous (186)

396. **DILATORY**

adj. <DIL-uh-tor-ee>

396. DILATORY

tending to delay; late or slow

It is easy to become **dilatory** in finishing your assignments during your first year of college.

397. **FRUGAL**

adj. <FROO-guhl>

397. FRUGAL

careful with money, stingy

Frugal Fran always brings a stack of coupons to the store.

398. **VIGILANT**

adj. <VIJ-uh-luhnt>

398. VIGILANT

alert; watchful

While walking on this road path, you must be **vigilant** and watch out for lions, tigers, and bears.

Synonyms: wary (178)

399. **ADULATION**

n. <AJ-uh-lay-tion>

399. ADULATION

excessive flattery

Stephanie has received so much **adulation** for her performance that it's just starting to annoy her.

Hip Hip Hooray!
laud (80), commend (121), extol (245), acclaim (307), adulation (399), exalt (402)

400. **ENERVATE**

v. <EN-er-vayt>

400. ENERVATE

to weaken or drain of energy

The soldiers were **enervated** after three straight days of heavy combat in the fields.

Synonyms: debilitate (118)

401. **IMPARTIAL**

adj. <im-PAHR-shuhl>

401. IMPARTIAL

fair; not biased

A judge must be **impartial** when presiding over a case.

Synonyms: objective (7), dispassionate (79)

402. **EXALT**

v. <eg-ZAWLT>

402. EXALT

to elevate, glorify, or praise

The eulogy **exalted** the noted scientist, claiming that his name will be remembered forever.

Hip Hip Hooray!
laud (80), commend (121), extol (245), acclaim (307), adulation (399), exalt (402)

403. **ABHOR**

v. <ab-HOR>

403. ABHOR

to hate

Bob **abhors** students who don't study.

Bad Blood
contempt (18), disdain (19), scorn (61), antagonistic (136), animosity (357), abhor (403), rancor (410), acrimony (467)

Word Alert: *Abhorrence* is the feeling of abhorring.

404. **GREGARIOUS**

adj. <gri-GAIR-ee-uhs>

404. GREGARIOUS

sociable

Gregarious Greg is always out among friends.

Synonyms: convivial (325)

405. **CEREBRAL**

adj. <suh-REE-brul>

405. CEREBRAL

intellectual

That movie is too **cerebral** for me; I prefer the Three Stooges.

406. **MERCENARY**

adj. <MUR-suh-ner-ee>

406. MERCENARY

motivated solely by a desire for monetary or material gain

I don't care if I seem **mercenary**; I refuse to help unless I get paid.

Word Alert: Mercenary can also be a noun meaning *one who works or serves for mercenary reasons.*

407. **TRANSITORY**

adj. <TRAN-si-tor-ee>

407. TRANSITORY

existing only briefly

True happiness can be achieved, but it is **transitory**, passing us by after the briefest of moments.

Gone with the Wind
elusive (84), evasive (172), ephemeral (287), transitory (407), transient (498)

408. **INTRANSIGENT**

adj. <in-TRAN-si-juhnt>

408. INTRANSIGENT

uncompromising, stubborn

If our boss remains **intransigent** about refusing to give us raises, we should go on strike.

Pig-Headed
tenacious (128), dogmatic (329), obstinate (337), intransigent (408), dogged (458), obdurate (465),

409. **INVIGORATE**

v. <in-VIG-uh-rayt>

409. INVIGORATE

to give life or energy to

Bob always feels **invigorated** after his morning cup of coffee.

410. **RANCOR**

n. <RANK-er>

410. RANCOR

hostility

The **rancor** between John and Scott is so great that they will never be friends again.

Bad Blood
contempt (18), disdain (19), scorn (61), antagonistic (136), animosity (357), abhor (403), rancor (410), acrimony (467)

411. CIRCUMVENT

v. <sur-kuhm-VENT>

411. CIRCUMVENT

to avoid or get around

In an effort to **circumvent** any delays, we skipped the middleman and went straight to the top.

Synonyms: elude [see elusive (84)], evade [see evasive (172)]

---

412. VERBOSE

adj. <ver-BOHS>

412. VERBOSE

using more words than necessary

Saying everything twice is unnecessary and **verbose**.
Saying everything twice is unnecessary and **verbose**.

Synonyms: bombastic (155), garrulous (469), voluble (478)

---

413. REPREHENSIBLE

adj. <rep-ri-HEN-suh-buhl>

413. REPREHENSIBLE

deserving of criticism or disapproval

John's actions are **reprehensible**; he attacked Scott and beat him senseless.

---

414. GRATUITOUS

adj. <gruh-TOO-i-tuhs>

414. GRATUITOUS

unnecessary

Sex and violence in a movie is only **gratuitous** if it doesn't advance the plot.

Synonyms: superfluous (280)

---

415. PRECIPITOUS

adj. <pri-SIP-i-tuhs>

415. PRECIPITOUS

extremely steep

You don't want to fall; it's a **precipitous** drop.

416. ABSTINENCE

n. <AB-stuh-nuhns>

416. ABSTINENCE

deliberate self-restraint

I am amazed at your **abstinence**; you haven't had any sweets in days.

417. FORTHRIGHT

adj. <FORTH-rite>

417. FORTHRIGHT

honest, direct, straightforward

Frank is always **forthright**, telling it like it is, no matter how painful the truth may be.

Synonyms: ingenuous (120), candid (124)

418. IMPEDE

v. <im-PEED>

418. IMPEDE

to be or get in the way of

I would have gotten here sooner but a stampede of cattle **impeded** my way.

Road Block
inhibit (177), hinder (183), thwart (272), hamper (297), encumbrance (301), impede (418)

Word Alert: An *impediment* is something that impedes.

419. INDICT

v. <in-DITE>

419. INDICT

to accuse of wrongdoing

John has been **indicted** for attacking Scott and is now awaiting trial.

420. USURP

v. <yoo-SURP>

420. USURP

to seize and take control without authority and possibly with force

The servants **usurped** power from their former masters.

421. **AMICABLE**

adj. <AM-ih-kuh-buhl>

421. AMICABLE

friendly

Known for its **amicable** atmosphere, Bob's Bar and Grill is a great place for friends to eat, drink, and be merry.

BFF
genial (218), amiable (262), affable (306), cordial (334), camaraderie (358), amicable (421)

422. **ASPIRE**

v. <uh-SPIRE>

422. ASPIRE

to have a great ambition

A-List students **aspire** to attend the nation's best colleges.

423. **GRATE**

v. (rhymes with "late")

423. GRATE

to irritate

His voice **grates** on me like fingernails scraping a chalkboard.

Synonyms: exasperate (154)

424. **MEAGER**

adj. <MEEG-er>

424. MEAGER

small, inadequate, or insufficient

This **meager** sandwich costs twenty dollars? What a rip off.

425. **REFUGE**

n. <REF-yooj>

425. REFUGE

protection or shelter

The refugees are seeking **refuge** from the war.

426. **CLAIRVOYANCE**

n. <klair-VOY-unss>

426. CLAIRVOYANCE

the power to see things that cannot be perceived by the senses

Fortune-tellers claim to possess **clairvoyance**.

Synonyms: prescience [prescient (304)]

---

427. **URBANE**

adj. <ur-BANE>

427. URBANE

polite, suave, and cultivated in manner

Bob is **urbane**, sophisticated, and simply the perfect gentleman.

---

428. **PROPRIETY**

n. <pruh-PRY-i-tee>

428. PROPRIETY

the quality of being proper

Discussing one's bowel troubles at the dinner table shows a lack of **propriety**.

Word Alert: If *im-* means *not*, what would *impropriety* mean?

---

429. **CAUSTIC**

adj. <KAW-stik>

429. CAUSTIC

harsh, stinging*;
sarcastic

Amy's **caustic** remarks really hurt John's feelings.

---

430. **DISCRETE**

adj. <di-SKREET>

430. DISCRETE

separate; distinct

The exam is made up of ten **discrete** sections that are each different from one another.

Word Alert: Don't confuse this word with *discreet* (222).

431. EXEMPLAR

adj. <ig-ZEM-pluh-ree>

431. EXEMPLAR

one who is worthy of imitation

Dylan is an **exemplar** of great scholarship; his articles are always extensively researched and coherently argued

Perfect 10
epitomize (104), paragon (256), exemplar (431)

Word Alert: To be *exemplary* is to be worthy of imitation.

432. COGENT

adj. <KOH-juhnt>

432. COGENT

forcefully convincing

The lawyer's **cogent** argument compelled the jury to find his client not guilty.

433. UNASSUMING

adj. <un-uh-SOO-ming>

433. UNASSUMING

not showy or arrogant; modest, plain

He is an **unassuming** worker, never making a scene over his accomplishments.

434. DELINEATE

v. <de-LIN-ee-ate>

434. DELINEATE

to depict or describe

The artist **delineated** the scene with startling accuracy.

435. CONTRITE

adj. <kon-TRITE>

435. CONTRITE

feeling or expressing remorse

The **contrite** student apologized for not studying her vocabulary.

Synonyms: penitent (492)

436. EFFACE

v. <ih-FACE>

436. EFFACE

to erase

The hypnotist successfully **effaced** any memory I had of that night.

437. SCOFF

v. (rhymes with "off")

437. SCOFF

to express or treat with disrespectful disregard

Scott **scoffed** at the question before him. "That's too easy. Give me a hard one!"

438. AUSPICIOUS

adj. <aw-SPISH-uhs>

438. AUSPICIOUS

favorable, successful

My trip to Vegas had an **auspicious** beginning: I hit the jackpot on the first slot machine I tried!

Word Alert: An *auspice* is auspicious sign.

439. EXACTING

adj. <eg-ZAK-ting>

439. EXACTING

requiring great care or effort

Writing a dictionary is an **exacting** task.

Synonyms: onerous (324)

440. DEPRECATE

v. <DEP-ruh-kate>

440. DEPRECATE

to mildly insult or belittle

She seemed polite at first, but she would constantly **deprecate** me with small condescending remarks.

Trash Talk

disparage (42), denounce (66), deride (77), decry (204), belittle (263), deprecate (440), vilify (485)

441. SCATHING

adj. <SKAYTHE-ing > (rhymes with "bathing")

441. SCATHING

harshly critical

The critic's **scathing** review of the movie convinced me not to watch it.

Thumbs Down
admonish (86), reproach (112), censure (213), scathing (441), rebuke (457), berate (486)

---

442. ELATED

adj. <ih-LAYT-ed>

442. ELATED

filled with delight

Franklin was **elated** with his 2400 on the SAT.

Happy Camper
sanguine (281), felicity (319), euphoria (354), ecstasy (365), elated (442), buoyant (449), mirth (481)

---

443. DESPONDENT

adj. <di-SPON-duhnt>

443. DESPONDENT

depressed, having no hope

Phil has become **despondent** over the loss of his job and spends his days sitting on the couch staring into space.

Cry Baby
melancholy (50), lament (51), despair (116), morose (284), despondent (443)

---

444. NEGLIGENT

adj. <NEG-li-juhnt>

444. NEGLIGENT

guilty of neglect

The **negligent** owner failed to feed his dog.

Word Alert: Don't confuse this word with negligible (395).

---

445. CONSOLIDATE

v. <kuhn-SOL-i-dayt>

445. CONSOLIDATE

to combine

It is a common practice for college graduates to **consolidate** all their school loans into one debt.

446. FEASIBLE

adj. <FEE-zuh-buhl>

446. FEASIBLE

possible, workable, practical

Your design for a flying car is great, but producing a car that expensive wouldn't be economically **feasible**.

447. SPORADIC

adj. <spuh-RAD-ik>

447. SPORADIC

occurring at irregular intervals

The enemy's attacks are too **sporadic**; we can't predict when the next one will occur.

448. CURSORY

adj. <KUR-suh-ree>

448. CURSORY

performed with haste and little attention to detail

A **cursory** effort when preparing for the SAT will yield nothing.

449. BUOYANT

adj. <BOY-ant>

449. BUOYANT

cheerful*;
capable of floating

The boy was so **buoyant**, he was bouncing up and down.

Happy Camper
sanguine (281), felicity (319), euphoria (354), ecstasy (365), elated (442), buoyant (449), mirth (481)

450. BRAZEN

adj. <BRAY-zuhn>

450. BRAZEN

rudely bold

That **brazen** brat gave me the finger!

451. **INTELLIGIBLE**

adj. <in-TEL-i-juh-buhl>

451. INTELLIGIBLE

capable of being understood

A good editor can turn an utterly convoluted manuscript into a perfectly **intelligible** masterpiece.

Word Alert: If the prefix *un-* means *not*, what would *unintelligible* mean?

---

452. **POMPOUS**

adj. <POM-puhs>

452. POMPOUS

overly self-important

"I'm bigger and bolder and rougher and tougher than anyone, sucker!" John exclaimed **pompously**. What a jerk.

Cocky
elitist (47), pretentious (52), condescend (117), grandiose (150), bombastic (155), patronize (356), pompous (452), haughty (463)

---

453. **BRUSQUE**

adj. (rhymes with "tusk")

453. BRUSQUE

rudely brief

"Shut up!" the boy said in a **brusque** manner.

---

454. **COMPOSED**

adj. <kuhm-POHZD>

454. COMPOSED

calm

Even as the plane was rapidly losing altitude the pilot remained **composed** and did not panic.

Chill
serene (142), tranquil (158), placid (164), composed (454), equanimity (476)

Word Alert: *Composure* is the state of being composed.
Word Alert: Composed also means *made up of.*

---

455. **ATROPHY**

v. <A-truh-fee>

455. ATROPHY

to waste away

If you do not exercise, you will **atrophy** into a weakling.

Word Alert: Atrophy can also be a noun meaning *a state of wasting away.*

456. LUXURIOUS

adj. <luhg-ZHOOR-ee-uhs>

456. LUXURIOUS

rich and superior in quality

The hotel's **luxurious** accommodations were fit for a king.

Overboard
extravagant (76), lavish (159), opulent (346), luxurious (456), exorbitant (471)

457. REBUKE

v. <ri-BYOOK>

457. REBUKE

to criticize or find fault with

The mother **rebuked** her child for peeing on the floor.

Thumbs Down
admonish (86), reproach (112), censure (213), scathing (441), rebuke (457), berate (486)

Word Alert: Rebuke can also be a noun meaning *an act or expression of criticism.*

458. DOGGED

adj. <DOG-ed>

458. DOGGED

stubbornly persevering

Though exhausted and severely dehydrated, Steve **doggedly** finished the marathon.

Pig-Headed
tenacious (128), dogmatic (329), obstinate (337), intransigent (408), dogged (458), obdurate (465),

459. ESPOUSE

v. <ih-SPOUZ>

459. ESPOUSE

to support

My spouse is very supportive and **espouses** every decision I make.

Synonyms: advocate (8)

460. TRITE

adj. (rhymes with "white")

460. TRITE

uninteresting because of overuse

With those **trite** pick-up lines, you'll never get a girl to give you the time of day.

Played Out
mundane (36), prosaic (194), banal (221), hackneyed (345), insipid (382), trite (460)

461. **VACILLATE**

v. <VAS-uh-layt>

461. VACILLATE

to be undecided, to hesitate

To be or not be? I keep **vacillating** between the two.

Synonyms: waver (343)

462. **EFFICACIOUS**

adj. <ef-i-KAY-shuhs>

462. EFFICACIOUS

effective

The **efficacious** treatment effectively cured my headache.

463. **HAUGHTY**

adj. <HAW-tee>

463. HAUGHTY

snobbish; overly proud

Harry always has a **haughty** expression on his face, clearly demonstrating how little he thinks of you.

Cocky
elitist (47), pretentious (52), condescend (117), grandiose (150), bombastic (155), patronize (356), pompous (452), haughty (463)

464. **ENCROACH**

v. <en-KROHCH>

464. ENCROACH

to advance beyond limits

By expanding your house, you're **encroaching** upon my property. Back off!

465. **OBDURATE**

adj. <OB-doo-rit>

465. OBDURATE

stubbornly persistent in wrongdoing

The **obdurate** child got sent to the principal's office for the fifth time this week.

Pig-Headed
tenacious (128), dogmatic (329), obstinate (337), intransigent (408), dogged (458), obdurate (465),

466. **FRENETIC**

adj. <fruh-NET-ik>

466. FRENETIC

wildly excited; frenzied; frantic

Freddie tore apart the living room in a **frenetic** search for the cash he had misplaced.

467. **ACRIMONY**

n. <AK-rih-moh-nee>

467. ACRIMONY

hostility

After the way she constantly mistreated and abused him John now only felt **acrimony** towards Amy.

Bad Blood
contempt (18), disdain (19), scorn (61), antagonistic (136), animosity (357), abhor (403), rancor (410), acrimony (467)

468. **BURGEON**

v. <BUR-juhn>

468. BURGEON

to grow

The **burgeoning** political movement is gaining a thousand followers every week.

Synonyms: flourish (105)

469. **GARRULOUS**

adj. <GAR-uh-lus or GAR-yoo-lus>

469. GARRULOUS

talkative

Gary is so **garrulous** that it seems like he's always got his phone to his ear.

Synonyms: verbose (412), voluble (478)

470. **TORPOR**

n. <TOR-per>

470. TORPOR

inactivity

Because he sat on the bench for almost the entire game, the second-string quarterback fell into a deep **torpor** and missed his chance to play.

Word Alert: To be *torpid* is to possess torpor.

471. EXORBITANT

adj. <eg-ZAWR-bi-tuhnt>

471. EXORBITANT

excessive

The **exorbitant** cost of rent in Manhattan drives many people to find more affordable housing in Brooklyn or Queens.

Overboard
extravagant (76), lavish (159), opulent (346), luxurious (456), exorbitant (471)

472. AMELIORATE

v. <uh-MEE-lee-uh-rayt>

472. AMELIORATE

to improve

Productivity at the factory went up after working conditions were **ameliorated.**

473. BANE

n. (rhymes wih "cane")

473. BANE

a cause of death or ruin

Carelessness is the **bane** of every student of the SAT.

Killer
pernicious (326), deleterious (380), bane (473)

474. INCORRIGIBLE

adj. <in-KOR-i-juh-buhl>

474. INCORRIGIBLE

incapable of being corrected or reformed

The **incorrigible** crook robbed a bank just two days after getting out of prison.

475. FLORID

adj. <FLOR-id>

475. FLORID

elaborately or excessively ornamented; flowery

He writes in a **florid** style, elaborately describing every detail of every scene.

Flashy
ornate (226), flamboyant (244), garish (374), florid (475)

476. **EQUANIMITY**

n. <eh-qua-NIH-mih-tee>

476. EQUANIMITY

calmness, mental or emotional stability

Scott is known for displaying **equanimity** in times of stress.

Chill
serene (142), tranquil (158), placid (164), composed (454), equanimity (476)

---

477. **AMENABLE**

adj. <uh-MEN-uh-buhl>

477. AMENABLE

open to advice or suggestion

She is in need of assistance and is **amenable** to any suggestions that you might have.

---

478. **VOLUBLE**

adj. <VOL-yuh-buhl>

478. VOLUBLE

characterized by ready and rapid speech

Our **voluble** tour guide talks too fast and says too much.

Synonyms: verbose (412), garrulous (469)

---

479. **AVARICE**

n. <AV-uh-riss>

479. AVARICE

greed

The lawyer's **avarice** was obvious; he went to great lengths to squeeze every penny out of his clients.

---

480. **INCISIVE**

adj. <in-SAHY-siv>

480. INCISIVE

penetrating, clear, and sharp

Unlike most baseball announcers, Steve gives truly **incisive** analysis instead of repeating the same hackneyed ideas.

Eagle Eye
discern (43), astute (96), keen (234), perspicacity (384), incisive (480)

481. **MIRTH**

n. (rhymes with "birth")

481. MIRTH

gladness, amusement, laughter

Janice brings **mirth** wherever she goes; she is always laughing and giggling, which puts everyone in a good mood.

Happy Camper
sanguine (281), felicity (319), euphoria (354), ecstasy (365), elated (442), buoyant (449), mirth (481)

---

482. **SUBVERT**

v. <suhb-VURT>

482. SUBVERT

to ruin;
to overthrow*

The protesters are planning to **subvert** the administration and take over the school.

Word Alert: Something *subversive* is intended or serving to subvert.

---

483. **PUGNACIOUS**

adj. <puhg-NAY-shuhs>

483. PUGNACIOUS

eager to fight

The **pugnacious** pug barked at anyone who tried to pet it.

Fight Club
contend (72), cantankerous (200), irate (236), belligerent (283), pugnacious (483)

---

484. **OFFICIOUS**

adj. <uh-FISH-uhs>

484. OFFICIOUS

overly eager in offering unwanted help

That **officious** salesman won't leave us alone even though we told him we didn't want his help.

Synonyms: obtrusive (487)

---

485. **VILIFY**

v. <VIL-uh-fahy>

485. VILIFY

to say bad things about, to make into a villain

The press utterly **vilified** the politician, making it seem as if he himself had caused the blackout.

Trash Talk
disparage (42), denounce (66), deride (77), decry (204), belittle (263), deprecate (440), vilify (485)

486. **BERATE**

v. <bi-RAYT>

486. BERATE

to criticize severely or angrily

I hate when my mom **berates** me for petty offenses.

Thumbs Down
admonish (86), reproach (112), censure (213), scathing (441), rebuke (457), berate (486)

487. **OBTRUSIVE**

adj. <uhb-TROO-siv>

487. OBTRUSIVE

sticking out, noticeable;
brash, meddling*

Doug's **obtrusive** behavior at the party shocked everyone when he loudly asked the hostess about her marital troubles right in the middle of dinner.

Synonyms: officious (484)

Word Alert: To *obtrude* is to be obtrusive.

488. **INSULAR**

adj. <IN-syu-ler>

488. INSULAR

isolated; narrow-minded

The islanders are an **insular** people who know nothing of the outside world and don't care to learn.

Synonyms: provincial (102)

489. **ASSIDUOUS**

adj. <uh-SIJ-oo-uhs>

489. ASSIDUOUS

hard working

The ass can be an **assiduous** animal; when properly motivated, it does a lot of work.

Synonyms: diligent (164)

490. **FACILITATE**

v. <fuh-SIL-i-tayt>

490. FACILITATE

to make easier

These new athletic facilities should **facilitate** local athletes' workout regimens.

Word Alert: Something *facile* is easy or done with little difficulty.

491. CIRCUITOUS

adj. <sur-KYOO-ih-tus>

491. CIRCUITOUS

being or taking a roundabout course

Instead of taking the highway, the bus driver took a **circuitous** route along windy side roads.

492. PENITENT

adj. <PEN-i-tuhnt>

492. PENITENT

feeling or expressing remorse

He is not at all **penitent** and refuses to apologize.

Synonyms: contrite (435)

Word Alert: *Penitence* is the state of being penitent. A *penance* is an act of penitence.

493. VOLUMINOUS

adj. <vuh-LOO-muh-nuhs>

493. VOLUMINOUS

big; having large volume

Her **voluminous** vocabulary is what allows her to be so voluble.

Synonyms: prodigious (309), copious (370)

494. SPECIOUS

adj. <SPEE-shus>

494. SPECIOUS

seemingly true but actually logically false

The lawyer's **specious** reasoning tricked the judge into dropping all charges against his guilty client.

Synonyms: spurious (335)

495. BUTTRESS

v. <BUH-tris>

495. BUTTRESS

to support or strengthen

The wall had to be **buttressed** so it wouldn't topple over.

Synonyms: bolster (74)

Word Alert: Buttress can also be a noun meaning *something used for support.*

496. **RECIPROCATE**

v. <ri-SIP-ruh-kayt>

496. RECIPROCATE

to show or give in return

If you'll scratch my back, I'll **reciprocate** and scratch yours.

497. **SPURN**

v. (rhymes with "burn")

497. SPURN

to reject with disrespect

Sarah **spurned** the bachelor's advances and then spit in his face.

498. **TRANSIENT**

adj. <TRAN-zee-uhnt>

498. TRANSIENT

existing only briefly

It turns out that John's feelings for Amy were **transient**: he has forgotten her and is now in love with Becky.

Gone with the Wind
elusive (84), evasive (172), ephemeral (287), transitory (407), transient (498)

499. **DISCORD**

n. <DIS-kawrd>

499. DISCORD

lack of agreement, quarreling

Their meetings were filled with **discord**; they just bickered with each other and got nothing done.

Word Alert: Something *discordant* is full of discord.

500. **LATENT**

adj. <LAY-tunt>

500. LATENT

existing in hidden or dormant form

She has always had a **latent** musical talent, but she is only now discovering it.

Appendix A: Numbered Word List

Here's a list of all the words in the order they appear in this book.

1 DISMISS
2 INNOVATIVE
3 SKEPTICAL
4 PROFOUND
5 ANECDOTE
6 UNDERMINE
7 OBJECTIVE
8 ADVOCATE
9 NOSTALGIA
10 INDIFFERENT
11 RESENT
12 COMPROMISE
13 CYNICAL
14 AESTHETIC
15 AMBIVALENT
16 EVOKE
17 DIMINISH
18 CONTEMPT
19 DISDAIN
20 PRAGMATIC
21 REVERE
22 PROVOCATIVE
23 INDULGE
24 RHETORIC
25 SCRUTINIZE
26 FOSTER
27 PLAUSIBLE
28 INACCESSIBLE
29 UNDERSCORE
30 AWE
31 SUBSTANTIATE
32 CONFORM
33 TRIVIAL
34 INDIGNATION
35 TEMPER
36 MUNDANE
37 VULNERABLE
38 APATHETIC
39 CREDIBLE
40 ARBITRARY
41 INHERENT
42 DISPARAGE
43 DISCERN
44 PROSPERITY
45 DIGRESS
46 PERPETUAL
47 ELITIST
48 ASSESS
49 PARADOX
50 MELANCHOLY
51 LAMENT
52 PRETENTIOUS
53 PARTISAN
54 AUTONOMY
55 AMBIGUOUS
56 PEDANTIC
57 COMPLACENT
58 NOVEL
59 REFUTE
60 IDIOSYNCRATIC
61 SCORN
62 OBSOLETE
63 DISCREDIT
64 INVOKE
65 ARTICULATE
66 DENOUNCE
67 DEFER
68 FUTILE
69 WHIMSICAL
70 INDUCE
71 ELOQUENT
72 CONTEND
73 UNIFORM
74 BOLSTER
75 COMPETENT
76 EXTRAVAGANT
77 DERIDE
78 EQUIVOCAL
79 DISPASSIONATE
80 LAUD
81 SOLEMN
82 HOMOGENEOUS
83 COLLABORATE
84 ELUSIVE
85 NOTORIOUS
86 ADMONISH
87 MEDIOCRE
88 CONSENSUS
89 ECCENTRIC
90 RETICENT
91 ERADICATE
92 METICULOUS
93 EMBELLISH
94 SUPPRESS
95 ORTHODOX
96 ASTUTE
97 ENIGMATIC
98 BENIGN
99 BENEVOLENT
100 PROLIFIC
101 COHERENT
102 PROVINCIAL
103 DEARTH
104 EPITOMIZE
105 FLOURISH
106 ZEALOUS
107 RECONCILE
108 EXPLOIT
109 SOMBER
110 DEBUNK
111 ADEPT
112 REPROACH
113 EXASPERATE
114 REMINISCE
115 DIVERGENT
116 DESPAIR
117 CONDESCEND
118 DEBILITATE
119 CONCILIATE
120 INGENUOUS
121 COMMEND
122 CONVOLUTED
123 VERSATILE
124 CANDID
125 CALLOUS
126 CONJECTURE
127 AFFLUENT
128 TENACIOUS
129 ESOTERIC
130 CAPRICIOUS
131 DUBIOUS
132 SUCCINCT
133 RESILIENT
134 INCONGRUOUS
135 MANIFEST
136 ANTAGONISTIC
137 ALIENATE
138 REITERATE
139 PRISTINE
140 EMPIRICAL
141 EMINENT
142 SERENE
143 HAIL
144 INCREDULOUS
145 CONFOUND
146 APPREHENSIVE
147 ENUMERATE
148 PREVALENT
149 OBLIVIOUS
150 GRANDIOSE
151 RESIGNATION
152 MAGNANIMOUS
153 BELIE
154 EXACERBATE
155 BOMBASTIC
156 ADROIT
157 INCONSEQUENTIAL
158 TRANQUIL
159 LAVISH
160 RESOLUTE
161 NONCHALANT
162 PLACID
163 OPPORTUNE
164 DILIGENT
165 SUPPLANT
166 MANDATE
167 PROLIFERATE
168 ERRATIC
169 INSOLENT
170 ANACHRONISTIC
171 GUILE
172 EVASIVE
173 DISPOSITION
174 PRECARIOUS
175 IMPETUOUS
176 CONCISE
177 INHIBIT
178 WARY
179 RECLUSIVE
180 ACCORD
181 PERVASIVE
182 ENCOMPASS
183 HINDER
184 SMUG
185 CONCEDE
186 FRIVOLOUS
187 EMULATE
188 WISTFUL
189 INNATE
190 EARNEST
191 DUPLICITY
192 EXPEDITE
193 OBFUSCATE
194 PROSAIC
195 REVOKE
196 RENOUNCE
197 STEADFAST
198 CACOPHONY
199 THERAPEUTIC
200 CANTANKEROUS
201 QUELL
202 AUSTERE
203 MOLLIFY
204 DECRY
205 ALTRUISTIC
206 CORROBORATE
207 CONCORD
208 ILLUSORY
209 SUBDUE
210 SOLICITOUS
211 ECLECTIC
212 EBULLIENT
213 CENSURE
214 AVERSE
215 DIFFIDENCE
216 JUXTAPOSE
217 VENERATE
218 GENIAL
219 CIRCUMSPECT
220 ASCERTAIN
221 BANAL
222 DISCREET
223 CONDONE
224 STOIC
225 DAUNT
226 ORNATE
227 EXUBERANT
228 PERSEVERE
229 RUDIMENTARY
230 INDIGENOUS
231 EUPHEMISM
232 ESTEEM
233 OMINOUS
234 KEEN
235 CARNIVOROUS
236 IRATE
237 DISPARITY
238 INNOCUOUS
239 DOCILE
240 ITINERANT
241 LUCID
242 EFFUSIVE
243 TERSE
244 FLAMBOYANT
245 EXTOL
246 STRIDENT
247 ABSTRUSE
248 TRACTABLE
249 ILLICIT
250 FERVENT
251 AMALGAM
252 PENCHANT
253 ARDOR
254 JADED
255 RELINQUISH
256 PARAGON
257 EXONERATE
258 FLAGRANT
259 DISSEMINATE
260 MITIGATE

261 CONSCIENTIOUS
262 AMIABLE
263 BELITTLE
264 JOCULAR
265 DECORUM
266 DISGRUNTLED
267 REPUDIATE
268 OPAQUE
269 CAJOLE
270 IMPASSIONED
271 ENTICE
272 THWART
273 DEMEAN
274 COMPEL
275 COMPLICITY
276 ARCHAIC
277 OBTUSE
278 LANGUID
279 CONCUR
280 SUPERFLUOUS
281 SANGUINE
282 POIGNANT
283 BELLIGERENT
284 MOROSE
285 TACT
286 COHESIVE
287 EPHEMERAL
288 DISCREPANCY
289 ARID
290 ESTRANGE
291 CONSTITUENT
292 WARRANT
293 ALLEVIATE
294 CIRCUMSCRIBE
295 CLANDESTINE
296 TACIT
297 HAMPER
298 IMPUGN
299 ABATE
300 OBSEQUIOUS
301 ENCUMBRANCE
302 PAUCITY
303 EULOGY
304 PRESCIENT
305 AUGMENT
306 AFFABLE
307 ACCLAIM
308 ALACRITY
309 PRODIGIOUS
310 PALLIATIVE
311 NEFARIOUS
312 ASCETIC
313 REDOLENT
314 CATHARTIC
315 ENTHRALL
316 MODICUM
317 PERTINENT
318 IMPERIOUS
319 FELICITY
320 INSTIGATE
321 VINDICATE
322 HEDONISTIC
323 INGRATIATING
324 ONEROUS
325 CONVIVIAL
326 PERNICIOUS
327 INSINUATE
328 SQUANDER
329 DOGMATIC
330 LACONIC
331 DIVISIVE
332 GALVANIZE
333 VAPID
334 CORDIAL
335 SPURIOUS
336 PRUDENT
337 OBSTINATE
338 DISPEL
339 ERUDITE
340 NEBULOUS
341 VOLATILE
342 VICARIOUS
343 WAVER
344 DETER
345 HACKNEYED
346 OPULENT
347 IMPECCABLE
348 POLARIZE
349 DISSENT
350 TUMULTUOUS
351 CONTRIVED
352 INQUISITIVE
353 JUDICIOUS
354 EUPHORIA
355 ENTRENCH
356 PATRONIZE
357 ANIMOSITY
358 CAMARADERIE
359 MUTABLE
360 CONSTRAIN
361 SURREPTITIOUS
362 CUNNING
363 VINDICTIVE
364 SCRUPULOUS
365 ECSTASY
366 SHREWD
367 STAGNANT
368 ADVERSITY
369 PLIABLE
370 PROPAGATE
371 ELUCIDATE
372 TREACHERY
373 HERETICAL
374 GARISH
375 CHRONIC
376 NURTURE
377 VEILED
378 AUDACITY
379 COPIOUS
380 DELETERIOUS
381 HARANGUE
382 INSIPID
383 INCONTROVERTIBLE
384 PERSPICACITY
385 DIVULGE
386 CURTAIL
387 MERCURIAL
388 TEDIOUS
389 OBSTREPEROUS
390 BOISTEROUS
391 PREDILECTION
392 INUNDATE
393 SAGACIOUS
394 PROPENSITY
395 NEGLIGIBLE
396 DILATORY
397 FRUGAL
398 VIGILANT
399 ADULATION
400 ENERVATE
401 IMPARTIAL
402 EXALT
403 ABHOR
404 GREGARIOUS
405 CEREBRAL
406 MERCENARY
407 TRANSITORY
408 INTRANSIGENT
409 INVIGORATE
410 RANCOR
411 CIRCUMVENT
412 VERBOSE
413 REPREHENSIBLE
414 GRATUITOUS
415 PRECIPITOUS
416 ABSTINENCE
417 FORTHRIGHT
418 IMPEDE
419 INDICT
420 USURP
421 AMICABLE
422 ASPIRE
423 GRATE
424 MEAGER
425 REFUGE
426 CLAIRVOYANCE
427 URBANE
428 PROPRIETY
429 CAUSTIC
430 DISCRETE
431 EXEMPLAR
432 COGENT
433 UNASSUMING
434 DELINEATE
435 CONTRITE
436 EFFACE
437 SCOFF
438 AUSPICIOUS
439 EXACTING
440 DEPRECATE
441 SCATHING
442 ELATED
443 DESPONDENT
444 NEGLIGENT
445 CONSOLIDATE
446 FEASIBLE
447 SPORADIC
448 CURSORY
449 BUOYANT
450 BRAZEN
451 INTELLIGIBLE
452 POMPOUS
453 BRUSQUE
454 COMPOSED
455 ATROPHY
456 LUXURIOUS
457 REBUKE
458 DOGGED
459 ESPOUSE
460 TRITE
461 VACILLATE
462 EFFICACIOUS
463 HAUGHTY
464 ENCROACH
465 OBDURATE
466 FRENETIC
467 ACRIMONY
468 BURGEON
469 GARRULOUS
470 TORPOR
471 EXORBITANT
472 AMELIORATE
473 BANE
474 INCORRIGIBLE
475 FLORID
476 EQUANIMITY
477 AMENABLE
478 VOLUBLE
479 AVARICE
480 INCISIVE
481 MIRTH
482 SUBVERT
483 PUGNACIOUS
484 OFFICIOUS
485 VILIFY
486 BERATE
487 OBTRUSIVE
488 INSULAR
489 ASSIDUOUS
490 FACILITATE
491 CIRCUITOUS
492 PENITENT
493 VOLUMINOUS
494 SPECIOUS
495 BUTTRESS
496 RECIPROCATE
497 SPURN
498 TRANSIENT
499 DISCORD
500 LATENT

Appendix B: Alphabetic Word List

Here's a list of all the words in alphabetical order.

299 ABATE
403 ABHOR
416 ABSTINENCE
247 ABSTRUSE
307 ACCLAIM
180 ACCORD
467 ACRIMONY
111 ADEPT
86 ADMONISH
156 ADROIT
399 ADULATION
368 ADVERSITY
8 ADVOCATE
14 AESTHETIC
306 AFFABLE
127 AFFLUENT
308 ALACRITY
137 ALIENATE
293 ALLEVIATE
205 ALTRUISTIC
251 AMALGAM
55 AMBIGUOUS
15 AMBIVALENT
472 AMELIORATE
477 AMENABLE
262 AMIABLE
421 AMICABLE
170 ANACHRONISTIC
5 ANECDOTE
357 ANIMOSITY
136 ANTAGONISTIC
38 APATHETIC
146 APPREHENSIVE
40 ARBITRARY
276 ARCHAIC
253 ARDOR
289 ARID
65 ARTICULATE
220 ASCERTAIN
312 ASCETIC
422 ASPIRE
48 ASSESS
489 ASSIDUOUS
96 ASTUTE
455 ATROPHY
378 AUDACITY
305 AUGMENT
438 AUSPICIOUS
202 AUSTERE
54 AUTONOMY
479 AVARICE
214 AVERSE
30 AWE
221 BANAL
473 BANE
153 BELIE
263 BELITTLE
283 BELLIGERENT
99 BENEVOLENT
98 BENIGN
486 BERATE
390 BOISTEROUS
74 BOLSTER
155 BOMBASTIC
450 BRAZEN
453 BRUSQUE
449 BUOYANT
468 BURGEON
495 BUTTRESS
198 CACOPHONY
269 CAJOLE
125 CALLOUS
358 CAMARADERIE
124 CANDID
200 CANTANKEROUS
130 CAPRICIOUS
235 CARNIVOROUS
314 CATHARTIC
429 CAUSTIC
213 CENSURE
405 CEREBRAL
375 CHRONIC
491 CIRCUITOUS
294 CIRCUMSCRIBE
219 CIRCUMSPECT
411 CIRCUMVENT
426 CLAIRVOYANCE
295 CLANDESTINE
432 COGENT
101 COHERENT
286 COHESIVE
83 COLLABORATE
121 COMMEND
274 COMPEL
75 COMPETENT
57 COMPLACENT
275 COMPLICITY
454 COMPOSED
12 COMPROMISE
185 CONCEDE
119 CONCILIATE
176 CONCISE
207 CONCORD
279 CONCUR
117 CONDESCEND
223 CONDONE
32 CONFORM
145 CONFOUND
126 CONJECTURE
261 CONSCIENTIOUS
88 CONSENSUS
445 CONSOLIDATE
291 CONSTITUENT
360 CONSTRAIN
18 CONTEMPT
72 CONTEND
435 CONTRITE
351 CONTRIVED
325 CONVIVIAL
122 CONVOLUTED
379 COPIOUS
334 CORDIAL
206 CORROBORATE
39 CREDIBLE
362 CUNNING
448 CURSORY
386 CURTAIL
13 CYNICAL
225 DAUNT
103 DEARTH
118 DEBILITATE
110 DEBUNK
265 DECORUM
204 DECRY
67 DEFER
380 DELETERIOUS
434 DELINEATE
273 DEMEAN
66 DENOUNCE
440 DEPRECATE
77 DERIDE
116 DESPAIR
443 DESPONDENT
344 DETER
215 DIFFIDENCE
45 DIGRESS
396 DILATORY
164 DILIGENT
17 DIMINISH
43 DISCERN
499 DISCORD
63 DISCREDIT
222 DISCREET
288 DISCREPANCY
430 DISCRETE
19 DISDAIN
266 DISGRUNTLED
1 DISMISS
42 DISPARAGE
237 DISPARITY
79 DISPASSIONATE
338 DISPEL
173 DISPOSITION
259 DISSEMINATE
349 DISSENT
115 DIVERGENT
331 DIVISIVE
385 DIVULGE
239 DOCILE
458 DOGGED
329 DOGMATIC
131 DUBIOUS
191 DUPLICITY
190 EARNEST
212 EBULLIENT
89 ECCENTRIC
211 ECLECTIC
365 ECSTASY
436 EFFACE
462 EFFICACIOUS
242 EFFUSIVE
442 ELATED
47 ELITIST
71 ELOQUENT
371 ELUCIDATE
84 ELUSIVE
93 EMBELLISH
141 EMINENT
140 EMPIRICAL
187 EMULATE
182 ENCOMPASS
464 ENCROACH
301 ENCUMBRANCE
400 ENERVATE
97 ENIGMATIC
315 ENTHRALL
271 ENTICE
355 ENTRENCH
147 ENUMERATE
287 EPHEMERAL
104 EPITOMIZE
476 EQUANIMITY
78 EQUIVOCAL
91 ERADICATE
168 ERRATIC
339 ERUDITE
129 ESOTERIC
459 ESPOUSE
232 ESTEEM
290 ESTRANGE
303 EULOGY
231 EUPHEMISM
354 EUPHORIA
172 EVASIVE
16 EVOKE
154 EXACERBATE
439 EXACTING
402 EXALT
113 EXASPERATE
431 EXEMPLAR
257 EXONERATE
471 EXORBITANT
192 EXPEDITE
108 EXPLOIT
245 EXTOL
76 EXTRAVAGANT
227 EXUBERANT
490 FACILITATE
446 FEASIBLE
319 FELICITY
250 FERVENT
258 FLAGRANT
244 FLAMBOYANT
475 FLORID
105 FLOURISH
417 FORTHRIGHT
26 FOSTER
466 FRENETIC
186 FRIVOLOUS
397 FRUGAL
68 FUTILE
332 GALVANIZE
374 GARISH
469 GARRULOUS
218 GENIAL
150 GRANDIOSE
423 GRATE
414 GRATUITOUS
404 GREGARIOUS
171 GUILE
345 HACKNEYED
143 HAIL
297 HAMPER
381 HARANGUE
463 HAUGHTY
322 HEDONISTIC
373 HERETICAL
183 HINDER
82 HOMOGENEOUS
60 IDIOSYNCRATIC

Appendix C: Category list

Here's a list of all the categories that appear on the cards, along with a list of the words that belong to the category and a description of the words' shared characteristics.

Category	Description	Words
Bad Blood	*Words related to hatred*	contempt (18), disdain (19), scorn (61), antagonistic (136), animosity (357), abhor (403), rancor (410), acrimony (467)
BFF	*Friendly words*	genial (218), amiable (262), affable (306), cordial (334), camaraderie (358), amicable (421)
Chill	*Words related to peacefulness*	serene (142), tranquil (158), placid (164), composed (454), equanimity (476)
Cocky	*Words about people who think they're better than you.*	elitist (47), pretentious (52), condescend (117), grandiose (150), bombastic (155), patronize (356), pompous (452), haughty (463)
Cry Baby	*Words related to sadness*	melancholy (50), lament (51), despair (116), morose (284), despondent (443)
Eagle Eye	*Words related to perceptiveness*	discern (43), astute (96), keen (234), perspicacity (384), incisive (480)
Feel Better	*Words about making things better.*	temper (35), mollify (203), mitigate (260), alleviate (293), palliative (310)
Fight Club	*Words related to hostility*	contend (72), cantankerous (200), irate (236), belligerent (283), pugnacious (483)
Flashy	*Showy, decorative words*	ornate (226), flamboyant (244), garish (374), florid (475)
Gone with the Wind	*Words for things that do not last long.*	elusive (84), evasive (172), ephemeral (287), transitory (407), transient (498)
Happy Camper	*Words related to happiness*	sanguine (281), felicity (319), euphoria (354), ecstasy (365), elated (442), buoyant (449), mirth (481)
Hip Hip Hooray!	*Words related to praise*	laud (80), commend (121), extol (245), acclaim (307), adulation (399), exalt (402)
Killer	*Words for harmful things*	pernicious (326), deleterious (380), bane (473)
Like-Minded	*Words related to agreement or similarity*	conform (32), uniform (73), consensus (88), accord (180), concord (207), concur (279)
Noise Pollution	*Words for loud things*	cacophony (198), strident (246), tumultuous (350), obstreperous (389), boisterous (390)
Old School	*Words for old things*	obsolete (62), archaic (276)
Overboard	*Words for excessiveness*	extravagant (76), lavish (159), opulent (346), luxurious (456), exorbitant (471)

Party Hearty!	*Words related to peppiness*	ebullient (212), exuberant (227)
Perfect 10	*Words for perfect things*	epitomize (104), paragon (256), exemplar (431)
Pig-Headed	*Words related to stubbornness*	tenacious (128), dogmatic (329), obstinate (337), intransigent (408), dogged (458), obdurate (465),
Played Out	*Words describing boring things*	mundane (36), prosaic (194), banal (221), hackneyed (345), insipid (382), trite (460)
Road Block	*Words related to stopping or preventing action.*	inhibit (177), hinder (183), thwart (272), hamper (297), encumbrance (301), impede (418)
Serious Business	*Serious words*	solemn (81), somber (109), earnest (190)
Shady	*Words for trickery*	guile (171), duplicity (191), cunning (362), treachery (372)
Thumbs Down	*Words for disapproval*	admonish (86), reproach (112), censure (213), scathing (441), rebuke (457), berate (486)
Tight-Lipped	*Words for being quiet or not speaking much*	reticent (90), succinct (132), concise (176),terse (243), laconic (330)
Trash Talk	*Words for saying bad things about something*	disparage (42), denounce (66), deride (77), decry (204), belittle (263), deprecate (440), vilify (485)
Unpredictable	*Words for changeable or random things*	arbitrary (40), whimsical (69), capricious (130), erratic (168), impetuous (175), volatile (341), mutable (359), mercurial (387)
What the--?	*Words for unknown or uncertain things*	ambiguous (55), equivocal (78), enigmatic (97), esoteric (129), abstruse (247), nebulous (340)
Wise Guy	*Words for wisdom or cautiousness*	circumspect (219), discreet (222), prudent (336), judicious (353), shrewd (366), sagacious (393)
X-treme Intensity!	*Words for strong feelings*	zealous (106), fervent (250), ardor (253), impassioned (270), galvanize (332)

Appendix D: New word worksheet

Just because a word isn't in the box doesn't mean you can't learn it! Use this space to track new words you learn. Write down the word and its definition, then try to write your own sentence using the word.

Word: ____________________ Definition: ____

Sentence: ____

Word: ____________________ Definition: ____

Sentence: ____

Word: ____________________ Definition: ____

Sentence: ____

Word: ____________________ Definition: ____

Sentence: ____

Word: ____________________ Definition: ____

Sentence: ____

Word: ____________________ Definition: ____

Sentence: ____

Word: ____________________ Definition: ____

Sentence: ____

Word: ____________________ Definition: ____

Sentence: ____

Word: ____________________ Definition: ____

Sentence: ____

Word: ____________________ Definition: ____

Sentence: ____

Word: ____________________ Definition: ____

Sentence: ____

Word: ____________________ Definition: ____

Sentence: ____

Word: ____________________ Definition: ____

Sentence: ____

Word: ____________________ Definition: ____

Sentence: ____

Word: ____________________ Definition: ____

Sentence: ____

Word: ____________________ Definition: ____

Sentence: ____

Word: ____________________ Definition: ____

Sentence: ____

Word: ____________________ Definition: ____

Sentence: ____

Word: ____________________ Definition: ____

Sentence: ____

Word: ____________________ Definition: ____

Sentence: ____

Word: ____________________ Definition: ____

Sentence: ____

Word: ____________________ Definition: ____

Sentence: ____

Word: ____________________ Definition: ____

Sentence: ____

Word: ____________________ Definition: ____

Sentence: ____

Word: ____________________ Definition: ____

Sentence: ____

Word: ____________________ Definition: ____

Sentence: ____

Word: ____________________ Definition: ____

Sentence: ____

Word: ____________________ Definition: ____

Sentence: ____

Word: ____________________ Definition: ____

Sentence: ____

Word: ____________________ Definition: ____

Sentence: ____

Word: ____________________ Definition: ____

Sentence: ____

Word: ____________________ Definition: ____

Sentence: ____

Word: ____________________ Definition: ____

Sentence: ____

Word: ____________________ Definition: ____

Sentence: ____

Word: ____________________ Definition: ____

Sentence: ____

Word: ____________________ Definition: ____

Sentence: ____

Word: ____________________ Definition: ____

Sentence: ____

Word: ____________________ Definition: ____

Sentence: ____

Word: ____________________ Definition: ____

Sentence: ____

Word: ____________________ Definition: ____

Sentence: ____

Word: ____________________ Definition: ____

Sentence: ____

Word: ____________________ Definition: ____

Sentence: ____

Word: ____________________ Definition: ____

Sentence: ____

Word: ____________________ Definition: ____

Sentence: ____

Word: ____________________ Definition: ____

Sentence: ____

Word: ____________________ Definition: ____

Sentence: ____

Word: ____________________ Definition: ____

Sentence: ____

Word: ____________________ Definition: ____

Sentence: ____

Word: ____________________ Definition: ____

Sentence: ____

Word: ____________________ Definition: ____

Sentence: ____

Word: ____________________ Definition: ____

Sentence: ____

Word: ____________________ Definition: ____

Sentence: ____

Word: ____________________ Definition: ____

Sentence: ____

Word: ____________________ Definition: ____

Sentence: ____

Word: ____________________ Definition: ____

Sentence: ____

Word: ____________________ Definition: ____

Sentence: ____

Word: ____________________ Definition: ____

Sentence: ____

Word: ____________________ Definition: ____

Sentence: ____

Word: ____________________ Definition: ____

Sentence: ____

Word: ____________________ Definition: ____

Sentence: ____

Word: ____________________ Definition: ____

Sentence: ____

Word: ____________________ Definition: ____

Sentence: ____

Word: ____________________ Definition: ____

Sentence: ____

Word: ____________________ Definition: ____

Sentence: ____

Word: ____________________ Definition: ____

Sentence: ____

Word: ____________________ Definition: ____

Sentence: ____

Word: ____________________ Definition: ____

Sentence: ____

Word: ____________________ Definition: ____

Sentence: ____

LaVergne, TN USA
09 September 2010
196206LV00005B/2/P

9 780615 399980